CITIx60 RECIPES

PARIS

Local Tastemakers Bring You 60 Recipes of the City

In Paris, food is never just food; it is culture, ritual, and romance.

Whether it's the aroma of warm croissants and freshly-baked baguettes drifting from a corner boulangerie, the clink of glasses along a café-lined boulevard, or markets unfolding at first light, its culinary scene is as much about atmosphere as it is about artistry — a balance of reverence for tradition and an appetite for reinvention.

CITIx60 Recipes invites you to travel through the city one dish at a time. Within these pages, chefs, restaurateurs, and tastemakers share 60 recipes that reflect the French capital's enduring classics and vibrant contemporary edge. Alongside them are personal recommendations of beloved neighbourhood bistros, hidden wine bars, and destination dining rooms — offering a curated path through Paris's rich gastronomic landscape.

Whether you're planning your next journey or longing to relive a recent one, this book brings Paris—and its unmistakable spirit—to your kitchen and table.

From the hustle and bustle of the morning marchés to the sacred ritual of the two-hour lunch, Paris's culinary culture is woven into daily life — and understanding its unwritten rules could transform you from mere tourist to temporary Parisien(ne). Whether you're browsing for seasonal fruit, decoding a menu full of unfamiliar terms or choosing the perfect cheese and wine pairing, here's a quick guide for navigating the city's culinary landscape with respect, curiosity, and a little more confidence.

A Taste of Paris: Markets, Menus & Manners

① The Rhythm of Les Marchés

The local markets or marchés in Paris operate on centuries-old schedules. Most run mornings only (7 a.m. to 2 p.m.) in the same locations their predecessors occupied decades ago. Arriving early means getting the first pick of produce, but dropping in after noon might net you better prices as vendors aim to sell out. Unlike supermarkets that stock the same fresh items year-round, these markets reflect the true rhythm of the seasons. Parisians shop with nature's calendar, building meals around what's at its peak as the produce simply tastes better (and costs less)!

What To Look Out For

Spring (March–May)
White asparagus, strawberries (Gariguettes), purple artichokes, baby lettuce varieties, fresh herbs (tarragon, chervil), fava beans, fresh peas, spring lamb.

Summer (June–August)
Heirloom tomatoes, stone fruits (peaches, apricots, cherries), melons (Charentais), zucchini flowers, green beans, fresh figs, berries.

Autumn (September–November)
Wild mushrooms (cèpes, girolles), grapes, pears, chestnuts, game (venison, boar), pumpkins, late tomatoes, apples.

Winter (December–February)
Citrus (blood oranges, clementines), leeks, celeriac, endives, oysters, root vegetables, truffles, winter greens (lamb's lettuce), preserved foods (dried beans, lentils, salted fish).

Market Etiquette

Bring change.
Most vendors take cards, but cash remains king at smaller stalls. Breaking a €50 note for a €2 purchase may earn you frowns, so carry small bills and coins.

Always greet first.
Say “Bonjour, Madame” or “"Bonjour, Monsieur” before asking prices or pointing at produce. Skip this and you could be considered rude.

Don't touch the produce.
Tell the vendor what you need for when you plan to eat/cook it and they will pick accordingly. They know what's ripe now and what needs a day or two.

Try some French.
Markets may be less English-friendly than restaurants, so basic phrases like “Je voudrais...” (I would like) and “C'est combien?” (How much?) help.

Tip: Buying cheese? You can ask to taste before buying. For bread, buy only what you will eat that day — French bread typically has no preservatives.

② *À Table*: The Art of Dining

While there are rules in French dining, they are not meant to intimidate. These customs have shaped Parisian meals for centuries to create a rhythm where everyone can relax and savour the moment. The good news? Most of it is just respect and common sense. Perfection is not the goal; effort is — and a warm greeting, an open mind, and real curiosity about the food will take you further than flawless etiquette ever could!

The Essentials

Book ahead.

Reservations are recommended, even at casual spots. Use TheFork online or call directly; walk-ins might work at 3pm or 6pm, but prime dinner slots book days ahead.

Say hello.

Walk in, make eye contact, say "Bonjour", and wait to be seated. When leaving, a cheerful "Au revoir, merci!" to the room is the gracious exit.

Settle in.

Meals may unfold in phases over 1.5–2 hours with 15–20 minutes between courses. You can't rush the kitchen, so just relax and enjoy!

Signal subtly.

Servers will not interrupt to check on you, so if you need something, make eye contact and raise your hand slightly. Never snap your fingers or say "Garçon".

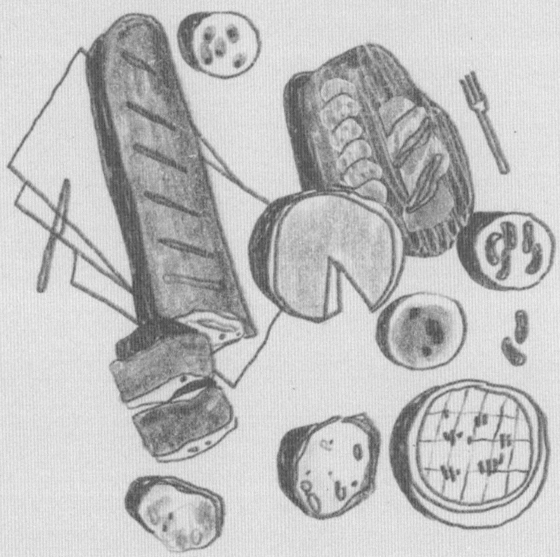

Request the bill.

It won't appear until you mime signing or say "L'addition, s'il vous plaît".

Tipping is optional.

While service is included, leaving €1–2 at cafés or rounding up 5–10% at restaurants has become slightly more common in tourist areas, but it's not expected.

Splitting the bill?

Mention it when you order. Most restaurants can accommodate separate checks, but it will be much smoother if they know upfront.

Once You're Seated

Keep your hands visible.
Rest both wrists on the table edge throughout the meal — not in your lap. It's a quirky remnant of medieval etiquette, but it's still the done thing.

Ask for water—it won't just appear.
Request "une carafe d'eau" (free tap) or "une bouteille d'eau" (bottled). Tap is what many locals go for.

Bread is your sidekick.
Tear it with your hands and use it to push food or mop up sauce. There won't be bread plates in traditional bistros so set it right on the tablecloth.

Fork stays in your non-dominant hand.
Follow the Continental style — keep the tines down and don't switch hands: use your knife (in your dominant hand) to guide food onto the back of the fork

Cheese before dessert.
It's a proper course — not a garnish or afterthought. When the server offers "Un peu de fromage?" or brings the cart, choose 3–5 cheeses yourself or ask them to compose a plate with variety: "Faites-moi une sélection, s'il vous plaît." If skipping cheese, go straight to dessert or coffee.

Trust the house wine (vin de maison).
It's chosen to complement the menu and represent the restaurant's taste, so ordering it is savvy — not settling. If the wine list overwhelms you, lean on your server by telling them what you like and your budget.

WINE ORDERING 101

"Un verre de rouge/blanc"
A glass of red/white

"Une carafe de vin rouge/blanc"
A carafe of red/white wine
(about 3 glasses)

"Une demi-carafe"
A half-carafe (good for 1–2 people)

"Une bouteille"
A full bottle (best value for 2+ people)

Coffee signals the end.
"Un café" (espresso) arrives after dessert to mark the meal's conclusion. Ordering it with your meal is a tourist tell — and cappuccinos/lattes are typically breakfast only.

When You Can't Eat Everything

While French cuisine often features meat, seafood and dairy, many menus now mark allergens (allergènes) and vegetarian/vegan-friendly spots are flourishing. That said, extensive modifications, off-menu requests, splitting dishes, or "on the side" substitutions are not standard practice, so if you have dietary restrictions, a little online research goes a long way.

SOME USEFUL PHRASES

"Je suis végétarien(ne)"
I'm vegetarian

"Je suis allergique aux..."
I'm allergic to...

"Sans gluten"
Gluten-free

"Il y a des noix dans ce plat?"
Are there nuts in this dish?

③ Decoding the Menu: Essential Terminology

French menus may look intimidating, but they are really just roadmaps once you crack the code. The language feels specific because French cooking is specific, with each method creating completely different textures and flavours. By learning a handful of key terms, you can stop second-guessing and start looking forward to each dish as it arrives on your table.

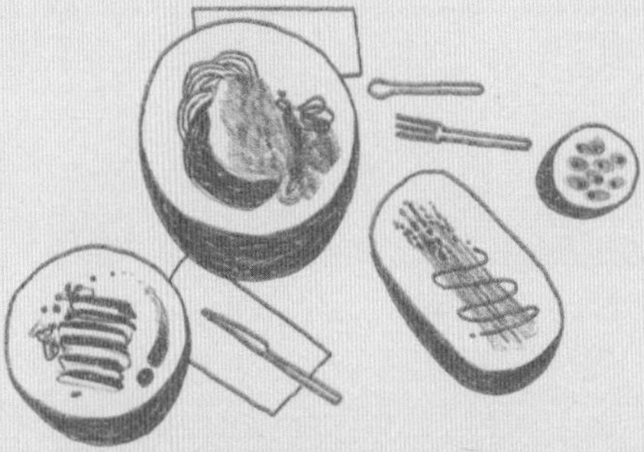

Your Meal Game Plan

THE ORDER

Starter
(Entrée)

↓

Main
(Plat)

↓

Cheese
(Fromage)

↓

Dessert

↓

Coffee
(Café)

WHICH MENU TO ORDER

La Formule
Set menu

Two or three courses at a fixed price, often the best value at lunch. Typically 2–3 choices are offered per course.

Prix Fixe / Menu du Jour
Fixed-price menu / Menu of the day

Similar to formule but often more elaborate, common at dinner and features seasonal ingredients.

À la Carte
By the card / From the menu

Individual dishes at individual prices as the more expensive but most flexible option.

Your Meat, Your Way

Bleu	Nearly raw, warm centre
Saignant	Rare, cool red centre
À point	Medium-rare, warm red centre (the standard)
Bien cuit	Medium to medium-well

Tip: The French don't do "well done" (très bien cuit) with quality cuts.

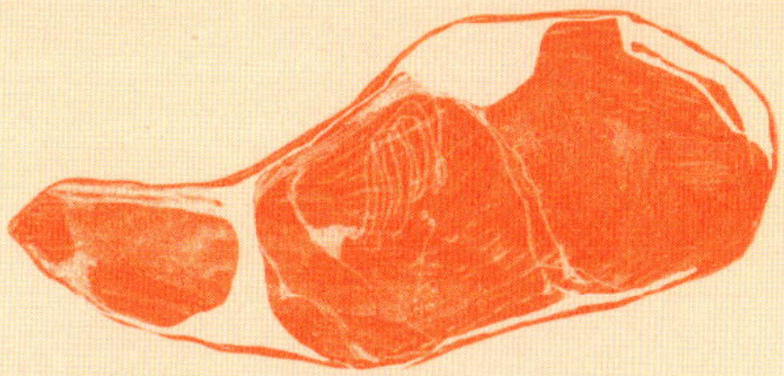

Don't Leave Without Trying...

Steak-frites	Steak with fries
Confit de canard	Duck leg slow-cooked in its own fat
Magret de canard	Duck breast, served pink
Boeuf bourguignon	Beef braised in red wine
Blanquette de veau	Veal in white cream sauce
Pot-au-feu	Boiled beef with vegetables
Andouillette	Tripe sausage
Ris de veau	Veal sweetbreads
Rognons	Kidneys
Foie de veau	Calf's liver
Boudin noir	Blood sausage

How It's Cooked

Poêlé	Pan-fried
Rôti	Roasted
Grillé	Grilled
Braisé	Braised
Confit	Slow-cooked in fat
En croute	In pastry
Fumé	Smoked
Cru	Raw
Mariné	Marinated

What's In That Sauce?

Béarnaise	Egg yolk, butter, tarragon, shallots
Au poivre	Peppercorn cream sauce
Bordelaise	Red wine and bone marrow
Beurre blanc	White wine and butter emulsion
Hollandaise	Egg yolk and butter emulsion

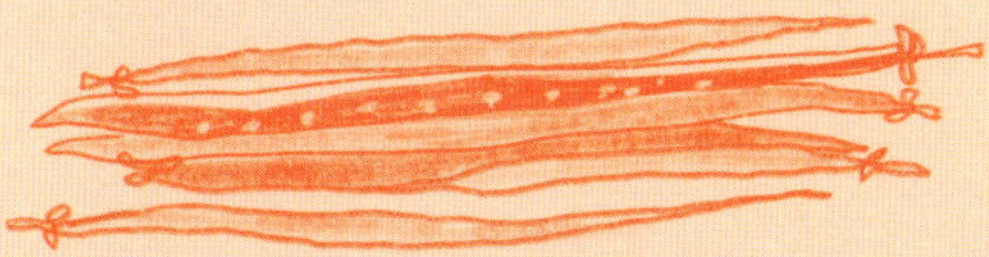

On The Side

Pommes frites	French fries
Gratin dauphinois	Scalloped potatoes with cream
Purée	Mashed potatoes (buttery, smooth)
Haricots verts	Green beans
Ratatouille	Provençal vegetable stew

60 Signature Recipes

From the heart of the city

Adam Purcell

Executive Chef, De Vie

Adam is an Irish chef from Dublin whose career has taken him through kitchens in Paris, London, and Copenhagen. His cooking is rooted in classical French training, heavily influenced by the creative food waste techniques he encountered in Copenhagen, and often includes a nod to the food he grew up with back home. Witnessing the scale of food waste in fine dining pushed him to adopt a circular approach to cooking, where by-products are seen as ingredients rather than something to be discarded.

Quick-Fire Question Round

Sweet or Savoury?
Surf, Turf or Greens?
Pasta or Rice?
Gourmet or Street Eats?
Baked, Fried or Grilled?

What is your go-to comfort food and why?
Tacos! (My husband is Mexican.)

What's a staple ingredient in your fridge?
As a chef, you'd think I'd have a well-stocked fridge, but it's actually quite the opposite. It's almost always empty — though I always make sure to have some good salted butter on hand.

What do you love about the food scene in your city?
You can find any cuisine, at any price point. Somewhere in Paris will always have exactly what you're in the mood for.

What is a dish that everyone should try at least once?
In Mexico, some restaurants and street vendors serve tacos de tripa — crispy pork intestines cooked on the plancha and served in a soft corn tortilla with salsa, raw onion, coriander, and a squeeze of lime. It's absolutely epic and a must-try when visiting Mexico.

What is your favourite food-related memory?
5-year-old me eating moules frites with my mum on a holiday to France.

Which restaurant in your city should visitors check out at least once?
It is actually just outside Paris but by far my favourite dining experience — Le Doyenée.

Asparagus & Aged Comté Tart, Smoked Brown Butter & Egg Yolk (01)

A seasonal dish that balances finesse with familiarity.

Yields 6 tarts

Shortcrust pastry

– T55 flour	200 g
– Cold unsalted butter, diced	100 g
– Fine salt	3 g
– Cold water	50 g

Comté béchamel

– Butter	45 g
– Flour	45 g
– Whole milk	600 ml
– Aged comté, finely grated	120 g
– Nutmeg, freshly grated	
– Fine salt	
– White pepper	

Smoked brown butter & egg yolk emulsion

– Cooked egg yolks	8
– Sherry vinegar	25 g
– Smoked brown butter	125 g
– Warm water, as needed	
– Fine salt	

Asparagus

– Green asparagus spears (large calibre)	12
– White asparagus spears (large calibre)	12
– Sunflower oil (for searing)	
– Extra virgin olive oil	
– Sea salt	
– Espelette pepper	

[1] **Shortcrust pastry:** Mix flour and salt in a bowl. Add cold butter and rub between your fingertips until the mixture resembles coarse crumbs. Add cold water and mix just until the dough comes together. Shape into a disk, wrap and refrigerate for at least 1 hour.

[2] **Tart shells:** Roll the dough to 2 mm thickness and line six 10 cm tart rings (about 55 g per shell). Trim edges and dock the base with a fork. Chill for 15 minutes, then line with parchment and baking beans. Bake at 170 °C for 12 minutes, remove the beans and bake for 5–6 minutes more until golden. Cool completely.

[3] **Comté béchamel:** Melt butter in a saucepan. Add flour and whisk for 2 minutes to form a roux. Gradually whisk in milk and cook until smooth and thick. Remove from heat, whisk in the comté until melted and season with salt, white pepper and nutmeg.

[4] **Smoked brown butter:** Cook 125 g of butter until the milk solids turn golden and aromatic. Transfer to a heatproof dish and smoke with smouldering hay in a covered container for 10–15 minutes. Strain.

[5] **Egg yolk emulsion:** Blend cooked yolks with sherry vinegar. Slowly drizzle in smoked brown butter to form a glossy emulsion, loosening with warm water if needed.

[6] **Asparagus:** Trim and peel asparagus. Blanch in salted boiling water until just tender, refresh in ice water and sear briefly in a hot pan to char slightly. Slice into rounds, reserving the tips.

[7] **To assemble:** Divide béchamel between tart shells. Arrange asparagus pieces upright, drizzle with olive oil and flash in a 180 °C oven for 2 minutes. Season with sea salt and Espelette pepper. Serve with a quenelle of the smoked brown butter egg yolk emulsion.

CHEF'S NOTE

The tarts can be made in advance. The final flash in the oven is not to cook it, as every element is already cooked. The idea is to warm it through and soften the béchamel.

Ayumi Sugiyama

Chef-owner, Accents Table Bourse

Born in Shizuoka, which is renowned for its mountainside tea fields, Ayumi trained in French pastry before crossing the world to settle in Paris in 2003 — where she worked in several pastry shops and gastronomic restaurants, including Stella Maris and La Truffière. In December 2016, she opened Accents Table Bourse as owner and pastry chef alongside her partner and chef, Romain Mahi. They earned their first Michelin star in 2019. In March 2025, the restaurant reopened with new decor inspired by raw nature.

Quick-Fire Question Round

Sweet or Savoury?

Surf, Turf or Greens?

Pasta or Rice?

Gourmet or Street Eats? I can't choose!

Baked, Fried or Grilled?

What is your go-to comfort food and why?
Miso soup with somen (thin Japanese noodles) because for breakfast, my mother prepared miso soup with leftover somen from the previous day. I love it!

What's a staple ingredient in your fridge?
Cabbage.

What do you love about the food scene in your city?
Dessert always completes the meal.

What is a dish that everyone should try at least once?
School canteen dishes in Japan.

What is cooking to you?
Pleasure.

Which restaurant in your city should visitors check out at least once?
Le Clarence helmed by chef Christophe Pelé.

p.195

Photo by Florian Domergue

Orange Chiffon Cake (02)

A light and elegant centrepiece for birthdays and afternoon tea.

- Egg yolks 120 g
- Milk 60 g
- Grapeseed oil 40 g
- Candied orange 50 g
- Flour 80 g
- Egg whites 200 g
- Sugar 100 g
- Cornflour 10 g

[1] Beat the egg whites, sugar, and cornflour to stiff peaks — whisk lines should be clearly visible and the meringue glossy.

[2] In a separate bowl, mix the egg yolks, milk, oil, and candied orange, then add flour.

[3] Fold in the meringue in three additions, using a whisk each time.

[4] Pour into an ungreased, unlined mould — the batter must cling to the sides.

[5] Bake in a fully preheated oven at 180 °C for 26 minutes. The cake is done when a light press on top produces no sound.

[6] Invert and cool completely in the mould before unmoulding with a small knife.

CHEF'S NOTE

This recipe is for a 21 cm-diameter cake mould.

Bertrand Chauveau

Chef-owner, Le Cornichon

Bertrand leads the kitchen at Le Cornichon, which focuses on flavourful, seasonal cuisine through hearty and generous dishes. His cooking balances accessibility with ambition: the weekly set menu runs like a neighbourhood canteen—simple and efficient—while his à la carte offerings are more elaborate, designed to turn an ordinary lunch into a proper Sunday feast. Through his skills and experience, he has created a convivial space where the food adapts to the moment.

What is a dish that everyone should try at least once?
Local specialties, as they always help us better understand where we are.

What is one thing you wish people understood about your culture's cuisine?
That the simplest things are often the most difficult.

What is your go-to comfort food and why?
Sweetbreads, for their delicacy and their indulgent appeal.

What's a staple ingredient in your fridge?
Semi-salted butter.

What do you love about the food scene in your city?
The diversity, and the ability of different players to constantly reinvent themselves — it challenges everyone and reminds us never to rest on our laurels.

What is your favourite food-related memory?
My grandmother's steak with parsley butter, fries, and tartar sauce.

What is cooking to you?
Giving pleasure.

Which restaurant in your city should visitors check out at least once?
Le Quincy.

Quick-Fire Question Round

Sweet or Savoury?

Surf, Turf or Greens?

Pasta or Rice?

Gourmet or Street Eats?

Baked, Fried or Grilled?

Photo by Nicolo Terraneo

Spanish-style Hake (Merlu à l'Espagnol) 03

A refined yet comforting spread for family Sunday lunches.

– Hake (for 2 pax)	500–700 g
– Tomatoes	5 kg
– Bell peppers	5 kg
– White onions	12
– Garlic	3 heads
– Tomato paste	500 g
– Salt	100 g
– Sweet paprika	50 g
– Hot chilli	10 g
– White vinegar	
– Olive oil	

[1] Clean and butterfly the hake, keeping the skin on.

[2] Grill skin-side down, then bake for 5 minutes in the oven covered with garlic slices.

[3] To make the basque sauce, place all ingredients in a Dutch oven, cover, and confit in the oven at 180 °C (356 °F) for 4 hours — then blend until smooth. The sauce yields approximately 30 servings.

[4] Separately, whisk together 60 g white vinegar and 140 g olive oil to make about 200 g of dressing for 2 servings.

[5] To serve, arrange the hake over the sauce and finish with a light drizzle of dressing.

CHEF'S NOTE

This Spanish-style hake is a nod to Hispanic cuisine, which is very close to ours.

Gazpacho Verde (04)

A refreshing starter for garden parties and tapas nights.

Gazpacho

– Zucchini	3300 g
– Celery stalks	500 g
– Basil	250 g
– Spring onions	500 g (1 bunch)
– Garlic	75 g
– Cucumber	1600 g
– Thyme	1 bunch
– Fine salt	75 g
– Red wine vinegar	300 g
– Balsamic vinegar	200 g
– Olive oil	700 g
– Green bell pepper	1500 g
– Shallots	100 g

Plating (1 pax)

– Gazpacho	200 g
– Celery brunoise	10 g
– Zucchini brunoise	10 g
– Chopped basil	10 g
– Croutons	10 g
– Chopped scallion	10 g
– Cucumber slices	20 g

[1] **Gazpacho:** Cut everything into a mirepoix, add the seasonings, mix well, and cover with plastic wrap directly in contact. Let marinate for 48 hours before blending.

[2] **Plating:** Mix the brunoises, season with salt and olive oil, and place them at the bottom of a soup plate. Cover with gazpacho, then arrange the cucumbers, croutons, and garnish with fresh basil leaves.

Asparagus with Mousseline Sauce (05)

Perfect for light summer entertaining and alfresco dining.

Mousseline sauce (for 30 pax)

– Egg yolks	130 g
– Smooth mustard	40 g
– Garlic purée	5 g
– Sunflower oil	450 g
– Cider vinegar	20 g
– Fromage blanc	300 g
– Sesame oil	80 g
– Salt	12 g
– Fennel seeds, powdered	1 g

Asparagus (for 1 pax)

– Asparagus (5–6 pieces)	150 g
– Sauce	40 g
– Tarragon, dill, parsley	
– Croutons	5 g

[1] Peel the asparagus and cook them in salted water (3%) for 3 minutes, then glaze.

[2] Trim the bases carefully so they sit cleanly on the plate.

[3] Brush with olive oil and season, then arrange.

CHEF'S NOTE

(Bottom) Asparagus with mousseline sauce is a Parisian reference — a classic bistro dish that can be found in many French households.

Claire Grumellon

Chef, Lissit

Quick-Fire Question Round

Sweet or Savoury?

Surf, Turf or Greens?

Pasta or Rice?

Gourmet or Street Eats?

Baked, Fried or Grilled?

Claire is a French chef renowned for her generous cuisine and charcuterie in Paris. After six years of diverse kitchen experience, she ran her own restaurant LE VAILLANT, where she reimagined bistro classics with a distinct personal touch. She has since joined Lissit, a bar-restaurant in the Oberkampf neighbourhood that pairs natural wines with traditional cuisine.

LISSIT p. 184

48 Rue de la Folie Méricourt, 75011 Paris   barlissit.com

What is your go-to comfort food and why?
Krishna Bhavan's Indian and vegetarian cuisine in the 10th arrondissement.

What's a staple ingredient in your fridge?
Cornichons.

What do you love about the food scene in your city?
It's diverse and pluralistic, attracting talent from all over the world and offering an exceptional supply of fresh produce.

What is a dish that everyone should try at least once?
Pâté en croûte (ours, haha!).

What is one thing you wish people understood about your culture's cuisine?
It's a kitchen that brings people together and is designed for spending long moments with those we love.

What is your favourite food-related memory?
Salted caramel crêpes in Saint-Malo while walking with my family.

What is cooking to you?
What drives me every day, my means of expression.

Which restaurant in your city should visitors check out at least once?
Quedubon 75019.

Photo by Louis Lepron

Tatin Boudin Poire (06)

Suited for rustic bistro-style meals with family and friends.

Pears	3000 g
Boudin (from your butcher)	800 g
Flour	200 g
Sugar for pastry (160 g for caramel)	35 g
Salt	20 g
Softened butter	115 g
Egg yolks	2
Milk	25 g

[1] Make a caramel and pour into the base of a mould lined with baking parchment.

[2] Peel, core, and slice the pears on a mandoline (~3 mm). Arrange over the caramel.

[3] Bake at 180 °C for 40 minutes, pressing the pears down into the mould every 10 minutes.

[4] Remove the skin from the boudin and shape into discs (5 cm diameter, 2 cm thick).

[5] Place the discs on top of the baked pears. Return to the oven for 10 minutes, then press down firmly.

[6] Make the pastry: combine flour, 35 g sugar, and salt. Add softened butter and work to a sandy texture. Add egg yolks and milk; knead by hand until a smooth ball forms.

[7] Roll the pastry and cut to the diameter of the mould. Lay over the boudin; spread evenly across the surface. Dock to prevent puffing. Bake for a further 20 minutes at 180 °C. Cool, then refrigerate for 3 hours.

[8] To serve, place a plate on top, invert, remove the mould and peel away the parchment.

CHEF'S NOTE

Serve with a simple lettuce salad dressed with a sharp vinaigrette.

David Kelly

Chef-owner, Project Sausage

David is a British chef and founder of Project Sausage, a British deli in Paris renowned for its handmade pies, Cornish pasties and gourmet sandwiches. After working in kitchens around the world, he settled in the French capital to champion modern British comfort food. His approach centres on quality and craft, introducing Parisians to the best of British baking.

PROJECT SAUSAGE p.176 57 Rue du Chemin Vert, 75011 Paris projectsausage.com

Quick-Fire Question Round

Sweet or Savoury? *All day long!*
Surf, Turf or Greens?
Pasta or Rice?
Gourmet or Street Eats?
Baked, Fried or Grilled?

What is your go-to comfort food and why?
One of our sausage rolls fresh out of the oven.

What's a staple ingredient in your fridge?
Crispy chilli oil or spiced BBQ sauce.

What do you love about the food scene in your city?
The variety available now plus the amazing ingredients being used.

What is a dish that everyone should try at least once?
Our scotch eggs on a Saturday morning.

What is one thing you wish people understood about your culture's cuisine?
That the reputation is not true. British cuisine has come on so much over the last few decades and is now so much better than before.

What is your favourite food-related memory?
I think my journey of discovery as a young cook working at Champneys health resort. From learning to cook right through to being chased around the kitchen with a lobster by the breakfast chef.

What is cooking to you?
My passion, a way to connect and express myself.

Which restaurant in your city should visitors check out at least once?
I highly recommend Towa for a special treat.

Scotch Eggs (07)

Well suited to pub-style breakfasts and relaxed family meals.

Serves 5 pax

– Sausage meat	500 g
– Organic eggs	6
– Extra eggs	2
– Flour	1 cup
– Dried Provençal herbs	1 tsp
– Dijon mustard	1 tsp
– Panko breadcrumbs	2 cup

[1] Bring a pan of salted water to the boil.

[2] Cook the organic eggs for 6 minutes, then transfer to iced water, then peel.

[3] Mix the dried herbs and mustard into the sausage meat. Weigh into 100 g balls and roll out between cling film into large circles.

[4] Wrap the sausage meat around the eggs and mould into egg shapes.

[5] Roll the eggs in in flour, then the beaten extra eggs, then the panko. Double-down on panko for extra crispiness.

[6] Deep-fry at 180 °C for 6 minutes — not for any longer.

Sausage Rolls (08)

Made for sharing, whether warm from the oven or packed for a picnic.

– Sausage meat	500 g
– Panko breadcrumbs	50 g
– Fresh sage	
– Pre-rolled puff pastry	
– Egg yolk	

[1] Preheat oven to 180 °C.

[2] Mix sausage meat, chopped sage, and panko in a mixer until combined. Portion into 95 g balls.

[3] Wrap each ball in puff pastry; pinch seams firmly to seal. Brush with egg yolk and place on a baking tray.

[4] Bake for 25–30 minutes, until puffed and golden brown.

CHEF'S NOTE

(Top) Every time I visited my grandma from Paris, I'd demand she make these! She used to sell them locally alongside her pies. When I started making them in Paris, they were an instant hit. We now make them every Saturday morning.

(Bottom) Use organic egg yolk for the best finish on the puff pastry.

Davide Luca

Chef-owner, Fimmina Pizzeria

Davide Luca, a Sicilian pizzaiolo who moved to Paris, discovered his passion for pizza at 14. At his restaurant Fimmina Pizzeria, he crafts contemporary, highly digestible pizzas with 72-hour fermentation, using only artisanal ingredients. His pink-toned space celebrates Italian femininity, simplicity, and the beauty of authentic, heartfelt cuisine.

Quick-Fire Question Round

Sweet or Savoury?

Surf, Turf or Greens?

Pasta or Rice?

Gourmet or Street Eats?

Baked, Fried or Grilled?

What is your go-to comfort food and why?
Pizza Margherita — simple, honest, and timeless. It reminds me of my beginnings in Sicily, where I learned that true comfort lies in quality and simplicity.

What's a staple ingredient in your fridge?
Good Italian olive oil — it gives soul to everything I cook.

What is cooking to you?
Cooking is a language — a way to tell who I am, where I come from, and what I love.

Which restaurant in your city should visitors check out at least once?
Fimmina Pizzeria.

Home-style Dough inspired by Fimmina

For light, fragrant pizza with a golden crust and airy crumb.

– Type 0 flour	700 g
– Type 1 flour	300 g
– Water	700 g
– Salt	25 g
– Extra virgin olive oil	25 ml
– Fresh yeast	2 g

[1] Create a biga by mixing 300 g flour, 135 g water, and 1 g fresh yeast into a rough dough (it should not be smooth). Cover and ferment 18 hours at 18 °C, until doubled with a slightly sweet and lactic smell.

[2] For the final dough, dissolve 1 g yeast in part of the water. Combine with the biga and remaining flour. Gradually add the rest of the water — and with the final small portion of water, add salt at the same time, then incorporate the olive oil. Knead until smooth and elastic.

[3] Rest 1 hour, covered — then divide into 280 g balls.

[4] Refrigerate them in sealed containers at 2–4 °C for 24 hours. Use once they are double in size — the perfect time to stretch the dough.

Note: Biga is a traditional Italian pre-ferment — a stiff mixture of flour, water, and a small amount of yeast fermented for 16–24 hours before being added to the final dough.

La Loren (09)

Ideal for casual gatherings with an elevated Italian touch.

- Pizza dough
- San Marzano tomato sauce
- Calabrian 'nduja
- Fresh fior di latte mozzarella
- Spicy salami, thinly sliced
- Buffalo stracciatella
- Fresh mint leaves
- Extra virgin oil

[1] Spread a thin layer of San Marzano tomato sauce over the pizza dough. See page 37 for dough recipe.

[2] Top with fior di latte mozzarella and small pieces of Calabrian 'nduja.

[3] Bake until the crust is golden and the toppings have melted.

[4] Add the spicy salami, buffalo stracciatella, and fresh mint leaves only once the pizza is out of the oven to preserve freshness and aroma.

[5] Finish with extra virgin olive oil.

La Tina (10)

Well suited to wine-and-pizza nights with a refined twist.

- Pizza dough
- San Marzano tomato sauce
- Fresh fior di latte mozzarella
- Fried purple eggplant chips
- Genovese-style basil pesto
- Buffalo mozzarella
- Fresh basil leaves
- Extra virgin olive oil

[1] Spread a thin layer of San Marzano tomato sauce over the pizza dough. See page 37 for dough recipe.

[2] Add fior di latte mozzarella evenly on top.

[3] Bake until the crust is golden and the cheese has melted.

[4] Once out of the oven, garnish with fried eggplant chips, dollops of pesto, buffalo mozzarella pieces, and fresh basil leaves.

[5] Finish with a drizzle of extra virgin olive oil.

CHEF'S NOTE

(Top) Inspired by the timeless charm of actress Sophia Loren, this pizza combines passion, strength, and bold southern flavours. It's fiery yet elegant — a balance between heat, creaminess, and freshness that mirrors the Italian spirit.

(Bottom) Use a high-quality tomato sauce such as San Marzano, violet eggplants, good extra virgin olive oil, and fresh, fragrant basil.

La Carrà (11)

A decadent harmony of smoke, sweetness, and depth.

- Fresh fior di latte mozzarella
- Gorgonzola cheese
- Smoked scamorza
- Warm Parmesan cream (added after baking)
- Lightly spicy fig jam
- Walnuts
- Extra virgin olive oil

[1] Evenly spread the fior di latte, gorgonzola, and smoked scamorza over the pizza dough. See page 37 for dough recipe.

[2] Bake until the crust is golden and the cheeses are fully melted.

[3] Remove from the oven and finish with warm Parmesan cream, a few drops of spicy fig jam, crushed walnuts, and a drizzle of extra virgin olive oil.

CHEF'S NOTE

Use a lightly spicy fig jam for a perfect contrast with the cheese blend. Add the Parmesan cream only after baking to preserve its smooth texture and aroma.

Davy Ngy

Owner, Distrito Francés

Davy's introduction to Mexican culture came through friends. With his Southeast Asian roots, the warmth and generosity of Mexican food felt instinctively familiar, but it was opening his first bottle of mezcal, during his early exploration of Mexican gastronomy, that truly sealed the connection — to the spirit itself, and to everything Mexico represents.

DISTRITO FRANCÉS

p. 176

10 Rue du Faubourg Saint-Martin, 75010 Paris
25 Rue du Pont Aux Choux, 75003 Paris · distritofrances.fr

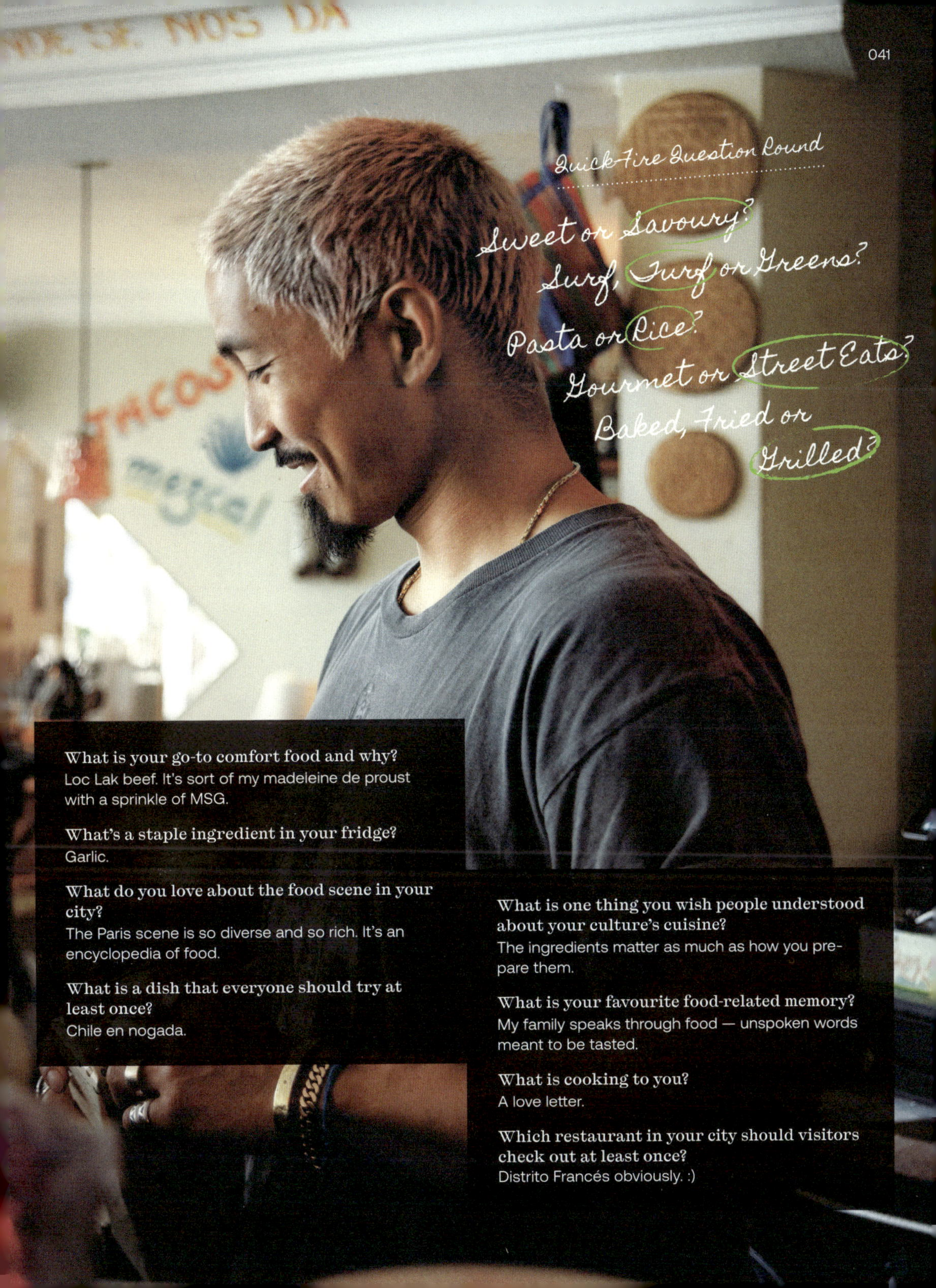

Quick-Fire Question Round

Sweet or Savoury?
Surf, Turf or Greens?
Pasta or Rice?
Gourmet or Street Eats?
Baked, Fried or Grilled?

What is your go-to comfort food and why?
Loc Lak beef. It's sort of my madeleine de proust with a sprinkle of MSG.

What's a staple ingredient in your fridge?
Garlic.

What do you love about the food scene in your city?
The Paris scene is so diverse and so rich. It's an encyclopedia of food.

What is a dish that everyone should try at least once?
Chile en nogada.

What is one thing you wish people understood about your culture's cuisine?
The ingredients matter as much as how you prepare them.

What is your favourite food-related memory?
My family speaks through food — unspoken words meant to be tasted.

What is cooking to you?
A love letter.

Which restaurant in your city should visitors check out at least once?
Distrito Francés obviously. :)

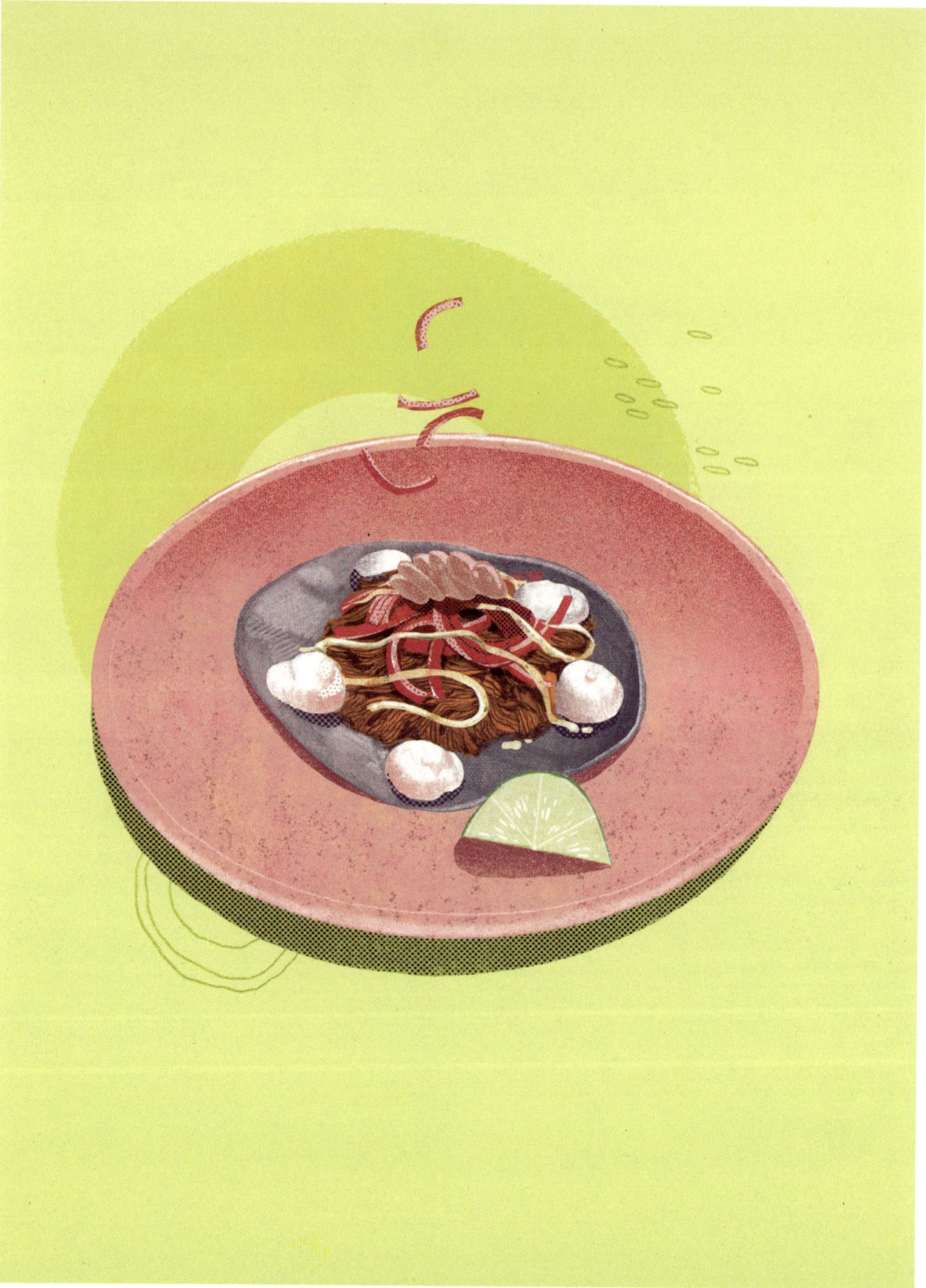

Daddy Yankee Carnita de Mole de Chile (12)

Perfect for festive get-togethers with bold flavours.

Serves 3 pax

– Pork shoulder	2 kg
– Garlic cloves	3
– Carrots	2
– Yellow onions	1.5
– Achiote	350 g
– Pasilla chilli	1
– Guajillo chilli	1
– Ancho chilli	1
– Habanero chilli	1
– Tomato concentrate	250 g
– Soy sauce	80 ml
– Paprika	8 g
– Cumin	8 g
– Pepper	8 g
– Honey	150 g
– Sugar	10 g
– Orange juice	200 ml
– Beer	250 ml
– Chipotle in adobo	10 g
– Mass harina (Naturelo)	150 g
– A pinch of salt	

[1] Boil the chillies. Remove the veins and seeds.

[2] Blend it with 200 ml of water, the achiote, chipotle in adobo, and orange juice until smooth.

[3] Cut the pork into pieces. Mince the garlic, onions, and carrot, then combine.

[4] Add the beer, soy sauce, tomato concentrate, paprika, cumin, and pepper.

[5] Mix everything by hand, then pour over the blended chilli sauce.

[6] Cover tightly with aluminium foil. Cook at 180 °C for 5 hours. Remove from the oven and shred everything.

[7] To make the tortillas, add tempered water to the masa harina little by little, mixing by hand until a ball forms. The dough should not be too wet.

[8] Divide into 8–10 balls, ping-pong ball size.

[9] Press into tortillas using a tortilla press and plastic sheets.

[10] Warm the tortillas in a pan and serve with the pork mixture.

CHEF'S NOTE

This is the dish I love to cook at family gatherings. Indulgent, with a good kick of spice — it's warm, fun and perfect for a taco party.

Ding Hélène

Co-founder, Red Katz

Quick-Fire Question Round

Sweet or Savoury?
Surf, Turf or Greens?
Pasta or Rice?
Gourmet or Street Eats?
Baked, Fried or Grilled?

Hélène grew up in a family where food shaped everyday life, anchoring moments and memories — especially New Year's celebrations, when the table overflowed with dishes, laughter, and warmth as her father cooked generously and her mother captured it all on film. Her father, a passionate restaurateur, passed on his love for the trade despite knowing its demands. Years later, she opened her own business while earning a culinary diploma in evening classes, driven by curiosity and the joy of transforming simple ingredients into sensory experiences rooted in love and tradition.

What is your go-to comfort food and why?
My go-to comfort food is Chinese food, because it's a cuisine meant for sharing. I love how dishes are placed in the centre of the table, inviting everyone to taste, exchange, and connect.

Which restaurant in your city should visitors check out at least once?
Relais de l'entrecôte.

What do you love about the food scene in your city?
The attention to presentation and refinement. Every dish feels carefully crafted, not only in flavour but also in how it looks on the plate. There's a sense of elegance and creativity that makes dining here a true experience.

What is a dish that everyone should try at least once?
Entrecôte. Perfectly seared, tender, and full of flavour, it's a true classic. There's something timeless about the balance between its simplicity and richness.

What is one thing you wish people understood about your culture's cuisine?
One thing I wish people understood about Chinese cuisine is that it's a balance of flavours, techniques, and stories. Every dish is a result of generations of practice, careful preparation, and respect for ingredients. Beyond being comforting, it's a cuisine that teaches patience, precision, and harmony, reflecting both the culture's history and its philosophy of sharing.

What's a staple ingredient in your fridge?
A staple ingredient in my fridge is meat. It's versatile and comforting, and I love how it can be prepared in so many different ways.

Photo by The Travel Buds

Stir-fried Ribeye with Black Pepper (13)

For sophisticated heat with the comfort of a shared meal.

Serves 3–4 pax

Steak

- Ribeye (entrecôte) 800 g
- Crushed black pepper 5 g
- Red bell pepper 1
- Green bell pepper 1
- King oyster mushrooms, thinly stripped 100 g
- Red onion, diced 50 g
- Minced garlic 4 g
- Oil 20 g
- Butter 15 g

Marinade

- Oyster sauce 24 g
- Sugar 5 g
- Homemade chicken stock cube 4 g
- Light soy sauce 32 g
- Chinese cooking wine 25 g
- Egg white 1
- Cornstarch 2 g
- A pinch of black pepper

Stir-fry sauce

- Homemade black pepper sauce 36 g
- Oyster sauce 36 g
- Sugar 18 g
- Homemade chicken stock cube 12 g
- Chinese cooking wine 48 g
- Light soy sauce 36 g
- Dark soy sauce 18 g

[1] Trim the ribeye and remove excess fat. Cut into even 2.5 cm cubes. Marinate for at least 3 hours. Dice the bell peppers and red onion into small cubes.

[2] Heat 20 g oil in a wok until very hot. Sear the marinated meat for 10–15 seconds. Remove and drain.

[3] Return the ribeye to the wok. Add crushed black pepper and minced garlic; stir-fry briefly to release the aromas. Add the diced vegetables and stir-fry for 50 seconds — just enough to cook them slightly but keep them crisp.

[4] Add the stir-fry sauce and 15 g butter. Give a final quick stir to coat the meat and vegetables.

[5] Serve immediately in a deep bowl. Arrange the meat and vegetables in the centre. Top with a few alfalfa sprouts for freshness and garnish with a pansy flower.

CHEF'S NOTE

Paris is famous for its high-quality meats like charolais and limousin. I use cubed entrecôte for this dish because it's a noble cut with just the right amount of fat, keeping it tender even in a wok. Don't shy away from marbling — it adds richness and enhances both taste and texture. Growing up, my father would make beef with peppers for the family, filling the kitchen with warmth and flavour. Inspired by those memories, I added a touch of butter to give a French twist to this Chinese-style dish — a harmony of tradition and innovation.

Fabrizio Rossi

Chef-owner, NEONATO

Fabrizio is a chef from Naples with a passion for cooking that started in childhood. He began his culinary journey in Paris nine years ago with Big Mamma, working his way through every position in the company. After gaining that breadth of experience, he opened NEONATO — a restaurant that reflects his Neapolitan roots, his creativity, and his commitment to authentic, contemporary Italian food.

182 Rue Saint-Martin, 75003 Paris neonatoparis.com

Quick-Fire Question Round

Sweet or Savoury?
Surf, Turf or Greens?
Pasta or Rice?
Gourmet or Street Eats?
Baked, Fried or Grilled?

What is your go-to comfort food and why?
I love Asian cuisine because it takes me out of my standards and comfort zone. It challenges me, surprises me, and pushes me to explore new flavours and techniques.

What's a staple ingredient in your fridge?
Piennolo's tomatoes and Salame Napoletano.

What do you love about the food scene in your city?
I love the variety and the quality. It's a great stage for chefs, with plenty of healthy competition that keeps everyone growing and improving.

What is a dish that everyone should try at least once?
Pasta e patate with provola or pasta e fagioli with mussels.

What is one thing you wish people understood about your culture's cuisine?
I wish people realised that Italian cuisine is much more than carbonara and pizza. It's a mosaic of regional traditions, each with its own unique ingredients, flavours, and stories — a reflection of Italy's true culinary soul.

What is your favourite food-related memory?
Parmigiana di melanzane.

What is cooking to you?
Cooking, for me, is a journey of discovery. It started with my roots in Naples, grew through my experiences in Paris, and became my voice at NEONATO — where tradition meets innovation on the plate.

Which restaurant in your city should visitors check out at least once?
NEONATO (Paris), Punta Tragara (Napoli).

Genovese D'anatra (14)

A soulful Neapolitan classic with depth and warmth.

Serves 3–4 pax

- Pasta (ziti spezzati di Gragnano)	400-500 g
- Duck meat	400 g
- Montoro onions (cipolla ramata di Montoro)	1 kg
- Taurasi red wine	500 g
- Bay leaves	2
- Celery	100 g
- Carrot	100 g
- Tomato paste	1 tbsp
- Fresh rosemary	10 g
- Extra virgin olive oil	100 g
- Salt	
- Pepper	

[1] Sear the duck meat and set aside.

[2] Heat olive oil in a large pot. Sauté the celery and carrot until fragrant. Add the onions and soften slowly.

[3] Deglaze with the red wine. Season with salt and pepper. Return the meat to the pot with the herbs and tomato paste.

[4] Cook gently over low heat for at least 6–7 hours until tender and deeply flavourful.

CHEF'S NOTE

This is a dish of humble art and patience — slow-cooked, bold, comforting, rooted in tradition and soul. Use cipolla ramata di Montoro if possible — its natural sweetness balances the richness of the duck and the depth of the Taurasi wine. Also, don't rush: slow cooking is key. The longer it simmers, the more harmonious the flavours become. A pinch of freshly ground coffee at the end lifts the aromas. You can also make this a day ahead — the sauce deepens overnight.

Pasta E Patate Con La Provola ⑮

Made for moments that call for warmth and generosity.

Serves 3–4 pax

– Short pasta (mezzi tubetti or ditali)	320 g
– Potatoes, peeled and diced	600 g
– Onion, finely chopped	1
– Celery, finely chopped	100 g
– Carrot, finely chopped	100 g
– Smoked provola cheese, diced	150 g
– Tomato paste	1 tbsp
– Grated Parmigiano Reggiano or Pecorino	40 g
– Extra virgin olive oil	2 tbsp
– Salt and black pepper to taste	100 g
– Fresh basil or rosemary (optional)	
– About 1 litre of vegetable broth or water	

[1] In a large pot, heat the olive oil and gently sauté the onion, celery, and carrot until soft and fragrant.

[2] Stir in the diced potatoes and cook for a few minutes, allowing them to absorb the flavours.

[3] Add the tomato paste, mix well, and pour in enough hot broth (or water) to cover the potatoes. Simmer for about 20–25 minutes, until the potatoes start to break down and create a creamy consistency.

[4] Add the pasta to the same pot and cook it risotto-style, stirring often and adding more broth as needed. The starch from the potatoes and pasta will create a thick, velvety sauce. Finish with the cheese.

[5] Once the pasta is al dente and the mixture is creamy, remove from heat. Stir in the diced smoked provola and grated cheese until perfectly melted and smooth. Adjust seasoning with salt and pepper.

[6] To serve, let it rest for a few minutes before serving. Garnish with fresh basil or a sprig of rosemary if desired. Serve warm and enjoy its comforting, rich texture.

CHEF'S NOTE

Top with 1–2 Parmesan rinds (Parmigiano Reggiano crusts).

Brodo in Tortelli Alla Cacciatora (16)

Rustic Italian flavours wrapped in tender, silken dough.

Serves 3–4 pax

Rabbit cacciatora

– Whole rabbit (about 1.2 kg), cut into pieces	1
– Onion, finely chopped	1
– Carrot, finely chopped	1
– Celery stalk, finely chopped	1
– Bay leaves	2
– Rosemary sprig	1
– Garlic clove	1
– White wine	200 ml
– Peeled tomatoes (or passata)	150 g
– Extra virgin olive oil	2 tbsp
– Salt and black pepper to taste	

Tortelli dough

– 00 flour	300 g
– Large eggs	3
– A pinch of salt	

Filling

– Concentrated rabbit cacciatora broth (from the braised rabbit)	300 ml
– 2 sheets of gelatin or 2 g agar-agar (to gelify the broth for easy filling)	

Sauce

– Braised rabbit meat (from the same preparation)	
– Cooking sauce	1 tbsp
– A drizzle of extra virgin olive oil	
– A few drops of rabbit jus (optional, for intensity)	

Cacciatora base:

[1] In a large pot, heat the olive oil and gently sauté onion, carrot, celery, garlic, and herbs until golden. Add the rabbit pieces, season, and brown on all sides. Deglaze with white wine and let it reduce. Add the tomatoes, a little water if needed, and cook slowly for about 1.5 to 2 hours, until the meat is tender and the sauce is rich.

[2] Remove the rabbit pieces and strain the sauce. Keep the meat warm. Reduce the sauce further until you obtain a concentrated, flavourful broth.

[3] Gelify the concentrated broth with gelatin or agar agar, let it set in the fridge, then cut into small cubes — this allows you to fill the tortelli without liquid spilling out.

Tortelli:

[4] Mix the flour, eggs, and a pinch of salt to form a smooth dough. Rest for 30 minutes, then roll it thin.

[5] Place small cubes of the gelified broth in the center of each pasta square, fold, and seal carefully to form tortelli. Keep refrigerated.

[6] Make the sauce by shredding the rabbit meat and mix it with a spoon of the braising sauce and a drizzle of olive oil. Warm gently until silky and glossy.

[7] Cook the tortelli in boiling salted water for 2–3 minutes. Drain carefully and glaze lightly with butter or olive oil. Plate the tortelli over a spoon of the rabbit sauce, finishing with a few drops of jus or herb oil if desired.

CHEF'S NOTE

For an aromatic finish, add burned rosemary.

Gregory Marchand

Chef-owner, Frenchie

Quick-Fire Question Round

Sweet or Savoury?

Surf, Turf or Greens?

Pasta or Rice?

Gourmet or Street Eats?

Baked, Fried or Grilled?

Greg started cooking at 15 in the kitchens of the Nantes orphanage where he grew up, then spent over a decade working across London, Hong Kong, Spain, and New York — where Jamie Oliver gave him the nickname "Frenchie" at Fifteen. Returning to Paris in 2009, he opened his first restaurant of the same name, followed by a wine bar, a street food spot, a wine shop, and eventually a London bistro. He then launched two more restaurants in Pigalle and Verbier (2020), Frenchie Biarritz inside the Regina Experimental Hotel (2023), and Altro Frenchie (2024). His approach is bold, generous, irreverent yet inspired — always open to the world and hungry for new encounters.

FRENCHIE p. 194 — 5 Rue du Nil, 75002 Paris — frenchie-ruedunil.com

FRENCHIE BAR À VINS p. 185 — 6 Rue du Nil, 75002 Paris — frenchie-bav.com

What is your go-to comfort food and why?
Sweetbreads cooked in brown butter, served with mashed potatoes and veal jus — simply because I love it.

What's a staple ingredient in your fridge?
I'm all about chilli sauce — all kinds, from all over the world. Harissa, homemade jamabanero, Sriracha... you name it. Every time I travel, I bring back a new bottle, and I put it on everything.

What do you love about the food scene in your city?
I love the diversity and accessibility of Paris — everything's so concentrated, the city is incredibly dense in the best way. And I'm especially into the whole natural wine bar scene happening here.

What is a dish that everyone should try at least once?
Bacon scones with maple syrup and raw cream — we serve them at Frenchie Bar à Vins.

What is one thing you wish people understood about your culture's cuisine?
The importance of saucing.

What is your favourite food-related memory?
When I came to New York for a trial at Gramercy Tavern in 2006, Chef Michael Anthony sat me at the bar and started sending out dishes. It was unlike anything I'd ever tasted before — this bold, flavourful, new American market cuisine, full of acidity, smokiness, and confidence. It left a mark.

What is cooking to you?
It's creating emotions through genuine hospitality.

Which restaurant in your city should visitors check out at least once?
Frenchie.

Photo by Offside

Guinea Fowl with Fresh Corn Polenta & Marinated Tomato (17)

A celebration of late summer, warmth, and garden freshness.

Serves 3–4 pax

– Guinea fowl (~2 kg)	1
– Fresh corn cobs	2
– Cherry tomatoes	6
– Garlic clove	1/2
– Lime (zest and juice)	1
– Lemon (juice)	1/2
– White balsamic vinegar	10 g
– Thyme sprig	1
– Popcorn kernels	12 g
– Shallot	1
– Flour	30 g
– Baby corn cobs	8
– Vegetable oil (for frying)	50 ml
– Poultry jus	100 g
– Basil and marjoram leaves	
– Thyme flowers	
– Olive oil	
– Butter	
– Salt	
– Fleur de sel	
– Espelette and black pepper	

Corn chips

– Cornmeal	30 g
– Milk	115 g
– Sugar	15 g
– Butter	10 g

[1] **Roast guinea fowl:** Preheat oven to 160 °C. Remove thighs and wings, leaving the breast on the carcass with skin intact. Season with olive oil and salt. Sear until golden, then roast for 14 minutes, turning every 3 minutes, to an internal temperature of 61 °C. Rest at least 20 minutes.

[2] **Fresh corn polenta:** Finely grate the corn to the core. Cook with lime juice and salt over medium heat until thickened. Off the heat, stir in butter (30 g). Keep warm.

[3] **Marinated tomatoes:** Halve tomatoes. Mix lemon juice, white balsamic, olive oil (20 g), garlic, thyme, and salt, then marinate 30 minutes.

[4] **Corn chips:** Preheat oven to 150 °C. Mix ingredients into a thick dough, then roll thin between Silpat and parchment. Cut 4 cm discs and bake about 14 minutes until golden then cool.

[5] **Popcorn crumble:** Pop kernels in a covered pan, then finely chop. Dice shallot (4 mm), dust with flour, and fry with vegetable oil until crisp. Drain and salt. Mix with popcorn and season with salt and Espelette pepper.

[6] **Roasted baby corn:** Sear in hot oil until well coloured. Season with lemon vinaigrette and fleur de sel.

[7] **To plate:** Spoon hot polenta onto the plate. Add baby corn, tomatoes, popcorn crumble, and corn chips. Slice guinea fowl thinly and arrange alongside. Finish with poultry jus, marjoram, basil, thyme flowers, lime zest, and adjust seasoning.

CHEF'S NOTE

I discovered corn in the US — back then in France, it was mostly used to feed pigs, canned corn aside. It was a revelation: incredible flavour, so sweet you could eat it raw. For me, corn marks the end of summer, the return from holidays. And this fresh corn polenta—grated and cooked at the last minute—is so much lighter than traditional polenta.

Hitoshi Minatani

Chef, Fugue

Hitoshi is a Japanese chef who lives in Paris. A devoted admirer of French gastronomy, he creates modern cuisine that bridges French culinary tradition and Asian culture.

128 Rue du Faubourg Saint-Martin, 75010 Paris   fugueparis.fr

Quick-Fire Question Round

Sweet or ~~Savoury~~? — **Savoury**

Surf, Turf or Greens?

Pasta or **Rice**?

Gourmet or **Street Eats**?

Baked, **Fried** or Grilled?

What is your go-to comfort food and why?
Ramen from Wagaya Ramen. Best ramen in town.

What's a staple ingredient in your fridge?
Garlic and shallots.

What do you love about the food scene in your city?
The global energy and the good balance between parks, nature, and old buildings.

What is a dish that everyone should try at least once?
Ramen (again, haha!).

What is one thing you wish people understood about your culture's cuisine?
I am just cooking to make people happy. This is the essence of why I am doing this. Pleasure before everything.

What is your favourite food-related memory?
Ayu, a small fish found only in Japanese rivers, traditionally cooked over a natural charcoal barbecue.

What is cooking to you?
Cooking is freedom and the best way to express myself.

Which restaurant in your city should visitors check out at least once?
Fugue, Pétrelle and Wagaya Ramen.

p.187

Red Mullet, Mussels, Risotto of Fregola & Spinach, Safran Sauce with Aïoli (18)

Ideal for celebratory gatherings with a Mediterranean touch.

Stock

– Fish bones and heads	
– Onion	1/2
– Celery stalk	1
– Fennel bulb	1
– Leek greens and parsley stems	
– Tomato paste	1 tbsp
– White wine	100 g
– Noilly Prat	50 g
– A splash of pastis	
– Fish or poultry stock	1 L
– Fennel seeds	1 tbsp
– Star anise	2
– A pinch of saffron	
– Sunflower oil	

Aïoli

– Sunflower oil	100 g
– Olive oil	100 g
– Garlic clove	1
– A pinch each of paprika and saffron	

Seafood & fregola

– Mussels	200 g
– White wine	50 g
– Shallot, finely sliced	1/2
– Thyme sprig	
– Butter	
– Fregola sarda	100 g
– Baby spinach	200 g
– Parmesan	20 g
– Olive oil	
– Red mullet fillets	3-4
– Tagetes flowers	
– Wasabi cress	
– Lemon juice	
– Chives	

[1] **Provençal fish stock:** Clean fish heads and bones under cold water, removing the eyes. Drain well. Heat sunflower oil in a large pan. Lightly brown the bones and heads. Add crushed garlic, onion, fennel, celery, and leek greens. Stir in tomato paste. Sauté for 5–10 minutes. Deglaze with white wine, pastis, and Noilly Prat. Add stock, bouquet garni, fennel seeds, and star anise. Bring to a boil, skim, and simmer 40 minutes. Pass through a food mill, then a fine chinois. Add saffron and reduce to one-fifth. Season with salt.

[2] **Aïoli:** Make a classic mayonnaise. Add grated garlic, paprika, and saffron, then mix until smooth.

[3] **Mussels:** Sauté the shallots in butter. Add mussels and white wine. Cover and cook over high heat until opened. Shell and set aside.

[4] **Red mullet:** Fillet the mullet. Cook gently in a pan over low heat for ~2 minutes per side, without browning. Tie the two fillets together with a chive strand for presentation.

[5] **Fregola risotto:** Cook the fregola according to package instructions, then drain. Blanch the spinach in salted boiling water and cool in ice water. Blend until smooth, then season. Combine the fregola, spinach coulis, Parmesan, and a few whole spinach leaves. Heat gently until creamy.

[6] **To serve:** Serve the red mullet over the spinach fregola risotto. Arrange mussels alongside. Spoon the reduced Provençal stock around. Finish with aïoli, tagetes flowers, wasabi cress, and lemon juice.

CHEF'S NOTE

This is a fish easily found in Japan, but no one eats it there. When I arrived in France, I discovered its taste and was fascinated. It has been my favourite thing to cook ever since. Be sure not to be stingy on the seasoning!

Jérémy Grosdidier

Chef-owner, Pristine & Vivide

Jérémy is a French chef from Nancy who trained in prestigious establishments, notably at Le Jules Verne in Paris, where he refined his precise and product-driven approach. Together with his partner Michelle Primc, he opened two restaurants in Paris, championing contemporary, locally sourced, and responsibly-minded cuisine.

PRISTINE — 8 Rue de Maubeuge, 75009 Paris — pristineparis.com

VIVIDE — 3 Rue Dancourt, 75018 Paris — vivide-paris.com

What is your go-to comfort food and why?
Pasta — it's easy and quick to prepare, and simple to adapt to the seasons.

What do you love about the food scene in your city?
The energy and fast-paced dynamic.

What is a dish that everyone should try at least once?
The smoked aerated butter we serve at Pristine.

What is one thing you wish people understood about your culture's cuisine?
That it comes with change — you can be inspired by traditional recipes and adjust them to today's approach to food.

What is your favourite food-related memory?
Any familiy meeting where there was food made with care.

What is cooking to you?
As cliché as it sounds, sharing — ideas, creativity, and the pleasure of eating together afterwards.

Which restaurant in your city should visitors check out at least once?
Septime, for its local produce, outstanding quality, and contemporary cuisine. p.195

Quick-Fire Question Round

Sweet or Savoury?
Surf, Turf or Greens?
Pasta or Rice?
Gourmet or Street Eats?
Baked, Fried or Grilled?

Photo by Jordan Sapally

Mushroom Tartelette (19)

For a comforting, refined and quietly indulgent treat.

Yields 4 tarts

Tarts

– Button mushrooms	400 g
– Onion	1
– Cream	150 ml
– Dry white wine	50 ml
– Tonka bean	1
– Fleur de sel	
– Freshly ground black pepper	
– A little fresh parsley	
– Puff pastry (fresh or from your favourite bakery)	1/2 sheet
– Toasted hazelnuts	10 g

Vinaigrette

– Honey	10 g
– Mustard	10 g
– Vinegar	20 g
– Oil	60 g

[1] **Mushroom duxelles:** Finely chop the onion and thinly slice 200 g of button mushrooms. Sauté the onion in a little fat, add the mushrooms, and cook until all moisture has evaporated. Deglaze with white wine, reduce, then season with fleur de sel, pepper, and chopped parsley. Set aside.

[2] **Tonka bean mushroom cream:** Cut the remaining 200 g mushrooms. Place in a saucepan with the cream and cover. Grate a small amount of tonka bean; use sparingly. Bake covered at 150 °C for 30 minutes. Blend until smooth, adjust seasoning and set aside.

[3] **Puff pastry:** Line the moulds with puff pastry. Prick the base with a fork. Cover with parchment and weigh down with dried lentils or baking beads. Blind bake at 190 °C for ~15 minutes. Cool slightly.

[4] **Mushroom salad:** Thinly slice the mushroom caps on a mandoline. Whisk together mustard, honey, and vinegar. Stream in the oil and add a little grated tonka bean.

[5] **To assemble:** Spread a layer of duxelle in each tart shell. Add a generous spoonful of mushroom cream. Arrange the mushroom salad on top for volume, then finish with a light drizzle of vinaigrette.

CHEF'S NOTE

Button mushrooms are called "champignons de Paris" in French; they were historically grown in the underground quarries of the city. Since opening Pristine, we've worked with an urban farm that grows mushrooms in an old parking lot in the 18th arrondissement to honour this tradition, with this recipe becoming a staple on our menu. Use the white caps for the salad and the trimmings for the duxelle and cream — nothing is wasted, and your salad will be beautifully white!

Julie Bavant

Chef-owner, Pistil

Quick-Fire Question Round

Sweet or Savoury? !!!

Surf, Turf or Greens?

Pasta or Rice?

Gourmet or Street Eats?

Baked, Fried or Grilled?

Julie is the founder of Pistil, a vegetarian restaurant tucked away in a hidden corner of Paris. Trained at l'Arpège, she is a passionate advocate of plant-based cuisine.

12 Rue Lechevin, 75011 Paris   pistil.paris

What is cooking to you?
It is sharing, and showing love.

Which restaurant in your city should visitors check out at least once?
Maslow Temple.

What is your go-to comfort food and why?
Any stew! It reminds me of my childhood.

What's a staple ingredient in your fridge?
Hot sauces and herbs.

What do you love about the food scene in your city?
It's very lively and vibrant, constantly adapting, and very inventive.

What is one thing you wish people understood about your culture's cuisine?
It's all about good products. The rest will follow if you choose your ingredients wisely.

What is your favourite food-related memory?
As a child, I used to fetch milk from the farmer, and my grandmother would always make me a sourdough tartine with the raw milk skin and fresh strawberries. Just like heaven!

Veggie Rillettes (20)

Well suited to convivial evenings with good bread and wine.

- Shallots 200 g
- King oyster mushrooms 200 g
- Smoked tofu 75 g
- Odourless coconut oil 100 g
- Salt
- Black pepper

[1] Peel and mince the shallots. Shred the mushrooms with a fork, following their length. Crush the tofu by hand.

[2] Heat half the oil in a pan. Fry the shallots gently until golden brown, season with salt. Set aside.

[3] In the same pan, add the remaining oil and cook the mushrooms until partly crisp and golden. Season with salt and pepper. Set aside to cool slightly.

[4] In a food processor, blend the tofu and shallots to a rough paste.

[5] Roughly chop the mushrooms — keep some pieces shredded for texture — and add to the paste.

[6] Season with salt and pepper, mix by hand until well combined. Transfer to a jar and chill for a couple of hours.

CHEF'S NOTE

As a child, I experienced big family tables — we were so many! There were always lots of starters, very meaty, like saucisson or rillettes, and I loved them so much I would feast on them and eat nothing else. My grandparents were mushroom mushrooms — keep some pieces shredded for texture — and I always had a thing for mushrooms. Growing up and cutting back on meat, I had to find a way to eat rillettes again. I came up with this recipe using mushrooms, and it tastes so real I don't miss the original anymore. Don't be shy with salt, pepper, and oil — they are essential to give this recipe the meaty feeling we are looking for. Always use whole black pepper and grind it yourself; it's a real game changer!

Louis Gallet

Head Chef, Terra

Louis is the Head Chef at Terra Restaurant in Paris. Originally from Savoie, he comes from a family of restaurateurs and has been passionate about food since childhood. One of his most vivid food memories is tasting freshly picked raspberries from the garden with his aunt — a moment that revealed to him the incredible intensity nature can offer. For Louis, cooking is about bringing out the very best in those products and pairing them with care. He shares his origins and memories through his cuisine, working closely with seasonal produce and the producers who supply the freshest ingredients.

TERRA p. 190 21 Rue des Gravilliers, 75003 Paris terraparis.fr

Quick-Fire Question Round

Sweet or Savoury?
Surf, Turf or Greens?
Pasta or Rice?
Gourmet or Street Eats?
Baked, Fried or Grilled?

What is your go-to comfort food and why?
Endive with ham is a dish we often had in my mother's kitchen and brings me comfort to this day.

What's a staple ingredient in your fridge?
I like to use chilli paste at home to spice up my dishes and take a break from our French classics.

What do you love about the food scene in your city?
The Parisian scene is very heterogeneous in terms of both gastronomy and population, which means that every week I discover new products, learn new methods and experience new tastes.

What is a dish that everyone should try at least once?
Blanquette de veau. A comforting dish that first appeared in the 19th century and was once served at bourgeois tables. Today, it's a grandmother's dish, where meat is seared and then simmered, with vegetables like leeks, carrots, mushrooms, and spring onions adding flavour to an elaborate sauce. It's a simple springtime dish that's brimming with know-how and love.

What is one thing you wish people understood about your culture's cuisine?
French cuisine is steeped in history. Every recipe we create is a journey through time — back to different moments in France's past, and to the childhood memories of our parents and grandparents, who honoured the land through the dishes that still bring us together today. It's a cuisine that's technical, indulgent, and precise. And while we celebrate its richness, we're equally committed to preserving the environment that makes it all possible.

Photo by Marie Potez

Pike Quenelle, King Prawn & Lobster Bisque ㉑

Perfect for dinners and festive gatherings with a classic touch.

Serves 4 pax

Bisque

– Olive oil	60 ml
– Lobster heads	600 g
– Small fennel bulb	1
– Leek, cleaned & sliced	1/2
– Small carrot, chopped	1
– Small yellow onion, chopped	1
– Head of garlic, cloves peeled	1/2
– Fennel seeds	1.5 g
– Cardamom pods	1 g
– Thyme sprig	1
– Rosemary sprig	1/2
– Cognac	20 ml
– Tomato paste	16 g
– Saffron threads	1 g
– Water	1.2 L
– Double cream	50 ml
– Cornflour (cornstarch)	2 g

Quenelle

– Pike or firm white fish flesh, finely chopped	400 g
– Whole eggs	4
– Egg whites	40 g
– Salt	6 g
– Double cream	40 g
– Unsalted butter	100 g
– Milk	52 ml
– Plain flour	104 g

Prawns

– King prawns or more if using smaller prawns	4

[1] **Homardine sauce:** Sweat the fennel, carrots, leeks, onions, garlic, thyme, rosemary, fennel seeds, and cardamom in olive oil. Once caramelised, remove the vegetables. Add more olive oil, then the lobster heads. Cook over high heat until they turn red. Stir in tomato paste and saffron, return the vegetables. Cook for 5 minutes. Deglaze with Cognac, cover with water, and simmer gently for 2 hours. Strain through a fine sieve and reduce by half. Add cream and boil for 10 minutes. Finish with a little cornstarch diluted in water to lightly thicken.

[2] **Quenelle:** Blend fish flesh, cream, egg whites, whole eggs, and salt in a food processor until smooth. Make the panade: combine milk, butter, and flour in a saucepan. Cook for 5 minutes, stirring constantly. Add to the fish mixture and blend again until completely smooth. Using cling film, form small, tightly sealed ballotines. Poach in simmering water for 10 minutes. Slice into rounds and sear in butter alongside the prawns.

[3] **To plate:** Arrange seared quenelle slices on the plate. Spoon the homardine sauce over, then top with the seared prawns.

CHEF'S NOTE

As an option, add a small sprig of tarragon — its aniseed notes pair beautifully with the richness of the dish.

Smoked Sea Trout, Peas, Trout Roe & Lemon Caviar (22)

Where sea and garden meet in refined harmony.

Serves 2 pax

– Trout fillets (80-100 g)	2
– Green peas	200 g
– Soft butter	100 g
– Finger lime (lemon caviar)	1
– Ponzu sauce	50 ml
– Olive oil	50 ml
– Lemon (yellow)	1
– Trout roe	40 g

[1] Lacquer the trout fillets with ponzu and olive oil.

[2] Cold smoke them with lemon wood and lemon peel, or add smoked oil or kororima berry to the lacquer. Lightly torch the visible side and finish with lime zest. Set aside.

[3] Shell the peas and blanch briefly in salted boiling water, then transfer immediately to an ice bath.

[4] Blend half the peas with 100 g butter until smooth to make the pea butter.

[5] Sauté the remaining peas briefly, add the pea butter, and warm through until well combined.

[6] To serve, spoon the pea mixture onto each plate, top with the trout, and finish with finger lime pearls and a teaspoon of trout roe.

CHEF'S NOTE

If you do not have the equipment at home to cold smoke the trout, smoked oil or kororima berry are great alternatives.

Manon Huguenin

Chef, Comptoir Club

Manon is a chef at Comptoir Club, a contemporary dining space defined by warmth and conviviality. Originally trained as a lawyer, she chose to leave that path behind to follow her true calling: cooking and the joy of sharing it. Today, she draws inspiration from exploring new ingredients and crafting unexpected combinations that surprise and delight, with vegetables holding a particularly special place in her cuisine. She is passionate about elevating and reinventing to make others happy through what they eat, offer comfort when needed, and introduce guests to flavours they may not yet have experienced to create moments that bring people together.

Quick-Fire Question Round

Sweet or Savoury?

Surf, Turf or Greens?

Pasta or Rice?

Gourmet or Street Eats?

Baked, Fried or Grilled?

What is your go-to comfort food and why?
My go-to comfort food is something I used to eat when I was a kid, which was a creation by my mom that she called "the flat rice". It's basically like a Spanish tortilla but made with brown rice and with some cheese and tomato sauce on top.

What's a staple ingredient in your fridge?
Mustard but not the classic Dijon mustard; the one with the mustard seeds which is a bit crunchy.

What do you love about the food scene in your city?
I love that the Parisian food scene is increasingly international while still respecting the traditional flavours of each cuisine. Dishes are not necessarily adapted to suit French tastes, allowing them to remain truly authentic.

What is a dish that everyone should try at least once?
If you come to Paris, I think you should try a good cordon bleu. It's a perfect example of French cuisine, made with quality ingredients that instantly transport you back to childhood.

What is one thing you wish people understood about your culture's cuisine?
French cuisine is not just food, but a way of life. To love cooking, to eat, to spend hours at the table with family and friends... To me, this is what French cuisine truly means.

Which restaurant in your city should visitors check out at least once?
Le Cyrano (17th) and Le Jourdain (20th).

Aioli, Sea Bream, Samphire Sauce & Vegetables (23)

Perfect for simple, seasonal celebrations shared around the table.

Serves 2–4 pax

Fish

– 4 sea bream filets or 2 sea bream	
– Carrots	4
– Potatoes	4
– Spring onions	4

Mayonnaise

– Garlic cloves	5
– Egg yolk	1
– Mustard	1 tbsp
– Seeded mustard	2 tbsp
– Sunflower oil	200 ml
– Xérès vinegar	3 tbsp

Samphire sauce

– Olive oil	1 cup
– Samphire	200 g
– A pinch of fleur de sel	
– A pinch of Espelette pepper	

[1] **Prep:** Peel the carrots and cut on the diagonal. Peel the potatoes and halve lengthwise. Halve the spring onions lengthwise. Bring a large pot of salted water to the boil. Cook the carrots and potatoes for 25 minutes; transfer to iced water. Repeat with the spring onions — 10 minutes, then ice.

[2] **Fish:** Preheat the oven to 180 °C. Fillet two sea bream to give four fillets. Lay on a baking tray, season with salt, Espelette pepper, and olive oil. Bake for 6 minutes — the fish should be just cooked and pearly.

[3] **Samphire sauce:** Bring a large pot of salted water to the boil. Blanch the samphire for 5 minutes; transfer to iced water. Blend with a cup of olive oil for 5 minutes until smooth.

[4] **Garlic mayonnaise:** Peel the garlic cloves. Heat gently in sunflower oil over low heat until caramel-coloured. Remove the cloves and reserve the infused oil for other uses. Whisk the egg yolk with the mustard. Gradually add sunflower oil in a thin stream, whisking continuously until thick. Finish with two tablespoons of sherry vinegar, and a little more oil if needed.

[5] **To serve:** Spoon the sauce onto the plate. Lay the sea bream fillet partially over the sauce. Arrange carrots, potatoes, and spring onions around and on top. Add a generous dollop of mayonnaise. Finish with olive oil, salt, and Espelette pepper.

CHEF'S NOTE

Aïoli is a traditional Provençal dish that reflects the culinary heritage and Mediterranean flavours of southern France. It's a festive meal often shared at family gatherings.

Egg Mayonnaise (24)

A classic addition to brunch tables and casual gatherings.

Serves 4 pax

– Eggs	8
– Egg yolk	1
– Mustard	1 tbsp
– Mustard with seeds	2 tbsp
– Sunflower oil	200 ml
– Xérès vinegar	3 tbsp
– Yellow mustard seeds	50 g
– Red cabbage	50 g
– Breadcrumbs	20 g
– Green oil	2 tbsp
– Sunflower oil	500 ml
– Greens of a bunch of spring onions to make the green oil	
– Smoked ground black pepper	1/4 tbsp
– A pinch of kosher salt	

[1] **Boiled eggs:** Bring a pot of water to the boil. Once boiling, gently add the eggs and cook for 8 minutes and 45 seconds. When done, immediately transfer the eggs to a bowl of cold water—ideally with ice cubes—to stop the cooking. Once cooled, peel the eggs.

[2] **Mayonnaise:** In a bowl, combine the egg yolk and the mustard. Start whisking, then gradually add the oil in a thin stream while continuing to whisk. Careful — the key to a successful mayonnaise is to add the oil very gradually. Once it begins to thicken, add the wholegrain mustard and the sherry vinegar. Continue adding the remaining oil until the mayonnaise reaches the desired consistency.

[3] **Pickles:** Mix 1 cup of brown sugar with 2 cups of sherry vinegar and 4 cups of water. Bring to a boil. Once boiling, pour the mixture over the sliced cabbage. Repeat the same process for the mustard seeds if you want to pickle them as well.

[4] **Breadcrumbs:** Use stale, dry bread and blend it until it becomes a fine powder. It's now ready to use.

[5] **Green oil:** Blend the green tops of the spring onions with oil. Strain through a fine sieve or muslin cloth to extract a smooth, vibrant green oil.

[6] **To serve:** Slice the eggs in half lengthwise — then place a small dab of mayonnaise on the bottom of your plate and add the eggs. Next, add a generous spoonful of mayonnaise on the yolk of each egg. Sprinkle with breadcrumbs, then add the pickled red cabbage and mustard seeds. Add a pinch of salt and Espelette pepper. Finish with a drizzle of green oil.

CHEF'S NOTE

For the breadcrumbs, simply use leftover bread, allow it to dry, then blend until fine. It's an easy way to add a little crunch to your eggs.

Boneless Pork Shoulder Roast, Potato Puree with Milky Onion Sauce (25)

A deeply comforting dish, made for slow afternoons and generous tables.

– Pork spare rib	1500 g
– White onions	500 g
– Milk	3 L
– Garlic	100 g
– Potatoes	1000 g
– Butter	125 g
– Salt	
– Pepper	

[1] Sear the pork roast in a very hot pan with some oil, then remove it and add the onions. Let the onions cook until they are caramelised.

[2] Place the pork roast in a rondeau with the milk, caramelised onions, thyme, salt and pepper. Cook on the hob over a low heat for about 5 hours OR in the oven for approximately 5 hours at 130 °C with 60% humidity.

[3] Peel the potatoes, cut them into large mirepoix-style chunks, then cook them in a large pot with water, along with salt and pepper. Once the potatoes are cooked, remove and mash them using a food mill, then add some butter and cream and mix.

[4] Once the roast is cooked, remove it and keep it warm.

[5] Recover the cooking milk and the onions, blend them together, then strain through a fine chinois. Reduce the mixture on low heat. Set some of the cooking milk aside.

[6] Finish the mashed potatoes by incorporating the cooking milk and folding in butter.

[7] Adjust the seasoning.

[8] To serve, slice the pork and place it in a serving dish. Pour the sauce on the pork and the mash potato into a bowl. Finish with some pepper and salt.

CHEF'S NOTE

For an extra smooth and flavourful mash, gradually incorporate the cooking milk while whisking vigorously, as if making an emulsion. This milk, infused with pork, onion, and thyme, adds a deep, savoury note that cream alone can't match. And if you really want to take it to the next level, pass the mash through a fine sieve for a texture worthy of a fine dining restaurant!

Marie-Lou Lizé

Co-founder, Nomie Spices

Quick-Fire Question Round

Sweet or Savoury?

Surf, Turf or Greens?

Pasta or Rice?

Gourmet or Street Eats?

Baked, Fried or Grilled?

Marie-Lou is co-founder of Nomie Spices, where she sources and blends spices from small-scale producers around the world. A passionate author, she writes to demystify spices and make them accessible and exciting for French cuisine, and she teaches regularly at La Source culinary school. She truly believes that life without spices is dull and flavourless. Having grown up surrounded by them, with her mother selling spices at a market for ten years, she learnt early on that quality spices can transform even the simplest dishes.

What is your go-to comfort food and why?
It's certainly my grandmother's gratin dauphinois, a recipe from my family's region near the Alps. The potatoes are slowly cooked in milk and cream, creating a texture that's soft and comforting like a hug. Nutmeg is the key companion to this dish, quite unusual in traditional French cuisine, which makes it even more special to me.

What's a staple ingredient in your fridge?
My must-have ingredient is harissa. We've created three versions: a mild one, a smoky one, and a very spicy green one. I use them as a base for vinaigrettes, in grilled cheese, to add a kick to mayonnaise, or even in pasta, like a pesto. I truly believe that life would be far too dull without harissa.

What do you love about the food scene in your city?
Paris is a vibrant city where all cultures find expression. Over the past 15 years, French cuisine has been reinventing itself, much to my delight; sweeping away the dusty standards of traditional gastronomy. Chefs are developing a genuine curiosity for cooking that is spiced, fiery, lively, and responsible. I feel incredibly fortunate to play an active role in this shift, supporting many chefs with our spices.

What is a dish that everyone should try at least once?
Salsa macha, a Mexican-inspired sauce created in collaboration with chef Carlos Moreno of Comer (10th). Originally from southern Mexico, this chili oil is traditionally made with dried chilies and fried garlic. Our version blends smoky chipotle and mild ancho chili, with dried mango for fruitiness, cashews and almonds for crunch and indulgence, and a touch of barberry for acidity. It elevates any dish and most often gets finished straight off the spoon!

Photo by Aurore Nguyen

Cauliflower Gratin with Tonka (26)

A familiar dish reimagined with quiet sophistication.

Serves 2–3 pax

– Large cauliflower	1
– Butter	40 g
– Flour	40 g
– Milk	500 ml
– Grated cheese (Comté, Gruyére or Parmesan)	70 g
– Tonka bean, finely grated	1
– Salt	
– Pepper	

[1] Preheat the oven to 180 °C (350 °F).

[2] Cut the cauliflower into florets and cook them in salted boiling water or steam for about 10 minutes — they should remain slightly firm.

[3] To make the béchamel, melt the butter in a saucepan, add the flour and stir. Gradually whisk in the milk to avoid lumps. Season with salt and pepper, then add the grated tonka bean (⅓ to 1/2 bean is enough).

[4] Place the cauliflower in a baking dish, cover with the béchamel, and sprinkle with grated cheese.

[5] Bake for 20–25 minutes, until golden and bubbling.

CHEF'S NOTE

Tonka bean is a truly exceptional spice — it enhances richness, supports it, and brings an incomparable lingering finish. I love its bitter almond notes, which pair beautifully with dairy. This dish also happens to be one of my five-year-old daughter's favourites.

Marine Gora

Chef-owner, Le Coyote

Marine is the founder of Le Coyote, a queer saloon in the heart of Paris's Marais district. After travelling to Montreal and discovering the history of Le Pulp — a legendary lesbian club that closed in 2007 — she set out to create a much-needed inclusive space for the LGBTQIA+ community and its allies. Drawing inspiration from cowboy aesthetics, Spanish counters, and Montreal bars like Spaghetti Western, she transformed the former Gramme 3 into a hybrid coffee shop, restaurant, and bar.

 p. 178

86 Rue des Archives, 75003 Paris @lecoyoteparis

What is a dish that everyone should try at least once?
Black pudding (from Basque Country with kintoa pork, the best one) — served with apples and mashed potato.

Which restaurant in your city should visitors check out at least once?
Brasserie Lipp in Saint Germain des Près.

What is your go-to comfort food and why?
A soup in general (phó, ramen, broth...).

What's a staple ingredient in your fridge?
My cousin's satay sauce.

What do you love about the food scene in your city?
It's really, really eclectic.

Quick-Fire Question Round

Sweet or Savoury? — I can't choose — I love both!

Surf, Turf or Greens?

Pasta or **Rice**?

Gourmet or **Street Eats**?

Baked, **Fried** or Grilled?

Scallop in the Shell (27)

Where ocean delicacy meets Southeast Asian vibrancy.

Serves 2 pax

– Roasted peanuts	
– Fresh garlic	
– Fresh chillies	
– Brown sugar (cassonade)	
– Oil	
– Butter	100 g
– Ginger	
– Lime	
– Dried scallop coral powder	
– Scallops, in the shell	2
– Kumquats	3

[1] **Coral butter:** Leave the butter at room temperature until soft. Blend with the coral powder, lime zest, ginger, smoked paprika, and a pinch of salt. Do not refrigerate.

[2] **Peanut sauce:** Roast the peanuts at 180 °C for 10 minutes. Break into pieces (not powder). Blend the garlic and chillies briefly, keeping some texture. Combine everything in a pan and cook very gently for 10–15 minutes until the garlic is soft.

[3] **To serve:** Sear the scallops and serve in the shell. Spoon the coral butter over the scallops, top with peanut sauce, and finish with sliced kumquats.

Coyote Cornbread (28)

Ideal for barbecues, outdoor feasts, and casual dinners.

– Melted butter	225 g
– All-purpose flour	240 g
– Yellow cornmeal (or polenta)	320 g
– Sugar	25 g
– Baking powder	20 g
– Baking soda	5 g
– Salt	6 g
– Buttermilk	675 g
– Large eggs	4
– Tartare sauce	
– Pickled chanterelles	
– Candied egg yolk	

[1] Preheat the oven to 200 °C (400 °F) with a rack in the middle. Lightly grease a 9-inch cast-iron skillet or baking dish and place it in the oven to heat.

[2] In a large bowl, whisk together the flour, cornmeal, sugar, baking powder (if using), baking soda, and salt. Make a well in the centre, add the buttermilk and eggs, and mix to combine. Stir in the slightly cooled melted butter and mix until just combined — do not overmix.

[3] Carefully remove the hot pan, pour in the batter (it should sizzle), and bake for 20–23 minutes, until golden and a toothpick inserted in the centre comes out clean. Cool for 10 minutes before slicing and serving with sauce, chanterelles and yolk.

CHEF'S NOTE

(Top) For this Vietnamese fusion dish, the idea is to use every part of the scallop especially during the height of scallop season — coral included. Don't be shy on the seasoning!

Mathilde Godement

Owner, Sandwichette

Mathilde is the owner of Sandwichette, a sandwich shop in Paris. She grew up in Normandy and spent her twenties travelling and eating her way around the world, torn between becoming a food journalist and a cook. Eventually, she opened her own shop to do both — and whatever else she fancies. She particularly loves inviting female chefs to create the sandwich of their dreams for pop-up collaborations. She loves bobby beans, peas, swimming, and cycling. An avid Oasis fan, she also plays guitar in her yet-unnamed punk girl band and has a black cat named Chatoune.

52 Rue Saint Maur, 75011 Paris sandwichette.com

Quick-Fire Question Round

Sweet or Savoury?

Surf, Turf or Greens?

Pasta or Rice?

Gourmet or Street Eats?

Definitively!

Baked, Fried or Grilled?

What is your go-to comfort food and why?
Anything that includes gluten and cheese.

What's a staple ingredient in your fridge?
Hot sauce, the best butter from Normandy and cheese, of course.

What do you love about the food scene in your city?
It's such a melting pot, you can taste and discover so many cultures with all the different restaurants in Paris.

What is a dish that everyone should try at least once?
Boeuf bourguignon..

What is one thing you wish people understood about your culture's cuisine?
That simple, great ingredients make the cuisine — no need for fuss. Seasonal produce is the key to success!

What is your favourite food-related memory?
When my grandpa picked a tiny strawberry from his garden and coated it with sugar and then gave it to me. I can still taste it ...

What is cooking to you?
Cooking is about feeding people — and it makes me feel good and free.

Which restaurant in your city should visitors check out at least once?
Le Baratin, Song Heng, Bang Bang and Le Servan.

p.185 p.182

Wild Garlic & Sausage Sandwich (29)

Comfort food with a springtime twist.

Serves 4 pax

Wild garlic	2 lb
Olive oil	2 cups
Sea salt	
Pork sausage	1 lb
Comté or good hard cheese	1 cup
Onions	1 cup
Black pepper	
Mustard	1 tsp
Good vinegar	1 tsp
Buns	4

[1] **Wild garlic pesto:** Wash and sort the wild garlic. Blend with olive oil, mustard, and vinegar. Season with salt, then set aside.

[2] **Sausage & onions:** Heat a little neutral oil in a skillet over medium heat. Add the sausage, removing from casings if needed, and cook until well browned and caramelised. Slice the onions finely into rings. Add to the pan, season with salt and pepper, and add a few fennel seeds if desired. Cook until soft and lightly golden, then set aside.

[3] **To assemble:** Slice the Comté thinly. Halve the buns and toast cut-side down in the same skillet until golden. Place the cheese on the warm buns and let it melt gently over low heat. Spoon the sausage and onion mixture over the melted cheese, add a touch of pesto, and close the sandwich. Serve warm.

Brown Butter & Black Vinegar Mayonnaise (30)

A condiment with character and depth.

Egg yolks	2
Dijon mustard	1 tsp
Sunflower oil	1 L
Salt	1 lb
Black vinegar	1 cup
Salted butter	113 g

[1] Mix the egg yolks with the mustard, then gradually add the oil in a thin, steady stream. The sauce will emulsify and thicken. Keep whisking at a consistent pace — not too fast or too slow.

[2] Once the mixture is thick and holds its shape, add the black vinegar and whisk to combine. Pour in the cooled brown butter (it must be cold) and continue whisking until smooth. Season with salt and pepper to taste.

CHEF'S NOTE

(Top) I used to live close to the woods where, during spring, I'd pick wild garlic — and bring back a lot of it. Making pesto was the best way to make it last. I've been playing with wild garlic ever since, and this is my favourite way to use it.

Chocolate & Vanilla Cake Marbré (31)

A tender sponge cake with ribbons of chocolate and vanilla.

Cocoa batter

– Melted butter, warm/cold	45 g
– White sugar	120 g
– Heavy cream	60 g
– Egg	50 g
– Flour	60 g
– Baking powder	1 g
– Cocoa powder	20 g

Vanilla batter

– Melted butter, warm/cold	50 g
– Whole egg	100 g
– White sugar	130 g
– Heavy cream	75 g
– Flour	120 g
– Baking powder	3 g
– Vanilla	3 g

Vanilla batter:

[1] Melt the butter and let it cool.

[2] Mix the eggs, sugar, and heavy cream together, then add the melted butter.

[3] Once the mixture is smooth and homogeneous, add the flour, baking powder, and vanilla. Set aside.

Cocoa batter:

[4] Mix the white sugar, heavy cream, and eggs, then add the cooled melted butter, and finally the flour, baking powder, and cocoa powder.

To assemble:

[5] Butter a rectangular loaf pan and line the bottom with a piece of parchment paper.

[6] Pour in a layer of about 2 cm of vanilla batter, then a 2 cm layer of cocoa batter, then another layer of vanilla batter, and so on until all the batter is used up.

[7] Bake at 170 °C (340 °F) for 40 minutes.

[8] Check doneness by inserting the tip of a knife — if it comes out clean, the cake is ready.

[9] Let it cool for about 10 minutes before removing it from the pan, then wrap it tightly in cling film.

[10] Enjoy it with ice cream, yoghurt or fruit for breakfast or simply as a a snack.

CHEF'S NOTE

Wrapping it helps keep all the moisture inside the cake, so it stays soft and doesn't dry out.

My-Ly Pham

Founder, BÀNỘI

My-Ly is the founder of BÀNỘI, a tiny canteen in Paris born from her reconnection with Vietnamese roots through travels across Southeast Asia Her signature spring rolls—filled with shrimp, salmon, lemongrass pork, or grilled tofu—blend traditional Vietnamese flavours with influences from neighbouring cuisines. Light, fragrant, and homemade, they reflect her modern take on Vietnamese street food in a cosy, welcoming space.

BÀNỘI p. 174 129 Rue Amelot, 75011 Paris 51 Rue des Vinaigriers, 75010 Paris banoi.fr

Quick-Fire Question Round

Sweet or Savoury?
Surf, Turf or Greens?
Pasta or Rice?
Gourmet or Street Eats?
Baked, Fried or Grilled?

What's a staple ingredient in your fridge?
Fresh herbs like mint and coriander; they're essential in Vietnamese cooking for their fragrance and balance.

What do you love about the food scene in your city?
Paris is a feast of contrasts: from street food to fine dining, the city has it all. You can travel the world just by walking down the street, and still find amazing food for every budget. Beyond that, Paris is renowned for its wine and bistronomic restaurants; it's what I miss the most whenever I travel abroad.

What is a dish that everyone should try at least once?
No visit is complete without a night of charcuterie and cheese, paired with good red wine and a crusty baguette.

What is one thing you wish people understood about your culture's cuisine?
Vietnamese food is all about harmony: sweet and sour, hot and cold, crunchy and soft. Balance is everything.

What is cooking to you?
Cooking is storytelling. It's how I share my roots and memories with others, one plate at a time.

Which restaurant in your city should visitors check out at least once?
If I have one restaurant to recommend, it's to try at least one traditional French brasserie, such as Brasserie Martin. Make sure to sit at the counter, where you can watch the chefs prepare some of the most classic dishes of French cuisine.

Vegetarian Spring Roll (32)

Perfect for lively gatherings and shared platters.

Serves 4–6 pax

Omelette

– Eggs	5
– Soy sauce	1 tsp
– Mirin	1 tsp
– Sugar	1 tsp
– Neutral oil for cooking	
– Salt	
– Pepper	

Caramelised onions

– Red onions	500 g
– Balsamic vinegar	3 tbsp
– Sugar	50 g
– Neutral oil for cooking	

Peanut sauce

– Garlic cloves, minced	2
– Piece of fresh ginger	1 cm
– Peanut butter	3 tbsp
– Hot water	4 tbsp
– Soy sauce	1.5 tbsp
– Rice vinegar	1 tbsp
– Sriracha	1 tbsp
– Honey	1 tbsp

Noodles & rolls

– Rice vermicelli (bun tuoi)	150 g
– Rice paper wrappers (22 cm)	12
– Avocado	1
– Crispy fried onions	50 g
– Fresh mint	1 bunch
– Fresh coriander	1 bunch
– 12 leaves of lettuce (batavia or similar)	

[1] **Omelette:** Beat the eggs with soy sauce, mirin, sugar, salt, and pepper. Pour into a hot, lightly oiled pan and cook gently, folding the edges in to keep it thick and slightly runny. Fold in half, cook briefly on both sides, then slice into 3 cm strips.

[2] **Caramelised onions:** Thinly slice the onions and sauté over high heat with oil. Once translucent, deglaze with balsamic vinegar. Lower the heat, add sugar, and simmer until completely reduced and caramelised (~15 minutes). Adjust seasoning accordingly.

[3] **Peanut sauce:** Combine all ingredients in a small saucepan. Heat and whisk until smooth, then strain.

[4] **Noodles:** Boil rice vermicelli for 4 minutes. Drain, rinse in cold water, and let dry until slightly sticky.

[5] **To assemble:** Dip a rice paper wrapper in warm water (~60 °C) for a few seconds. On the lower third, place avocado, omelette, caramelised onion, fried onion, lettuce, mint, coriander, and noodles. Fold the bottom over the filling, tuck in the sides, and roll tightly. Serve with the peanut sauce for dipping.

CHEF'S NOTE

Always place the prettiest ingredients (like avocado and the omelette) against the rice paper so they show through. Serve with the peanut sauce for dipping.

Pandan Chiffon Cake (33)

A gentle and fragrant dessert that comforts and uplifts.

<u>Serves 6–8 pax</u>

– Egg whites	5
– Egg yolks	3
– Sugar	90 g
– Sunflower oil	54 ml
– Coconut milk	63 ml
– Pandan extract	1 tsp
– Cornstarch	20 g
– Flour	60 g
– Baking soda	1/2 tsp
– Salt	1/4 tsp

[1] Preheat the oven to 180 °C (350 °F).

[2] Beat the egg whites with a pinch of salt. Once foamy, add two-thirds of the sugar and continue until stiff peaks form.

[3] In another bowl, mix egg yolks with the remaining sugar, oil, coconut milk, pandan extract, cornstarch, flour, and baking soda until smooth.

[4] Gently fold the egg whites into the batter.

[5] Pour into muffin moulds, filling about three-quarters full. Tap lightly to remove air bubbles.

[6] Bake for 20 minutes until risen and lightly golden.

CHEF'S NOTE

Let the cakes cool completely before removing from the moulds to preserve their fluffy texture.

Nicolas Ricouard

Chef-owner, Kamo & Tempête

Nicolas spent a decade in professional kitchens before opening his own restaurants. He trained at Le Mary Celeste, a natural wine and oyster bar where he worked with fish and global ingredients, eventually becoming head chef. Ready to build something from the ground up, he opened Tempête then Kamo two years later, and added two more restaurants in 2025.

KAMO — 17 Rue Martel, 75010 Paris — @kamo_paris

TEMPÊTE — 5 Cour des Petites Écuries, 75010 Paris — tempeteparis.fr

Quick-Fire Question Round

Sweet or Savoury? Tamarin

Surf, Turf or **Greens**?

Pasta or **Rice**?

Gourmet or **Street Eats**?

Baked, Fried or **Grilled**?

What is your go-to comfort food and why?
Spicy Sichuan noodles, especially the hand-cut "knife-cut" noodles from Mian Guan in Paris Belleville.

What's a staple ingredient in your fridge?
Cantabrian anchovies, guindillas, and a special chilli oil from the brand Anchao.

What is a dish that everyone should try at least once?
İskender kebab from a traditional Kurdish kitchen.

What is one thing you wish people understood about your culture's cuisine?
Cooking has no boundaries, but sometimes you have to respect the traditional way of serving it.

What is your favourite food-related memory?
My grandmother used to make a very simple sponge cake with orange blossom water. I have the recipe somewhere, and should work on it to feature it in one of our restaurants.

Which restaurant in your city should visitors check out at least once?
When I have time to eat out, I usually go to Le Verre Volé, Café du Coin (p.182), Cheval d'Or (p.179), Moko Loko, or Le Dauphin (p.188). For a fast, good French brasserie, head to Terminus Nord. Special mention to my favourites: Le Rigmarole (p.192), 19 Saint-Roch, and Maison Sota (p.188).

Sichuan Beef Cheeks (34)

Tender, melting texture balanced by vibrant heat and fragrance.

Meat

- Beef cheek or short ribs — 3 kg
- Onions — 2
- Carrots — 2
- Leek — 1

Marinade

- Light soy sauce — 80 g
- Dark soy sauce — 45 g
- 200 g Shaoxing wine or 1 bottle white wine
- Palm sugar or crystal sugar — 60 g
- Salt — 10 g
- Flour — 50-100 g
- Cinnamon sticks — 2
- Star anise — 5
- White pepper — 5 g
- Toasted sesame oil — 20 g
- Whole orange, peeled — 1
- Ginger, sliced — 1 piece
- Garlic cloves — 6
- Lemongrass stalk, smashed — 1
- Cornflour or rice flour — ~100 g

Sichuan sauce

- Soy sauce — 150 g
- Black rice vinegar — 90 g
- Sugar — 40 g
- Chilli oil — 175 g
- Sichuan pepper — 14 g
- Toasted sesame oil — 25 g
- Gochujang — 50 g
- Fermented black beans — 50 g
- Cornstarch or potato starch — ~100 g

[1] Dust the beef cheek with flour — this is important for a thick sauce later. Season with salt and oil. Sear in a hot pan until coloured on all sides, then set aside. Deglaze the pan with a glass of water to lift all the flavour from the bottom.

[2] Place the seared beef in a large pot or oven dish. Add all the marinade ingredients along with the carrots, leeks, and onions, roughly cut; they will cook for hours, so keep them large. Mix everything together, cover, and refrigerate overnight. The wine will help tenderise the meat.

[3] The next morning, top up with water to cover. Cook on a low heat on the stove with a lid for 41/2–5 hours, or in the oven at 120 °C, also covered, for the same time.

[4] Carefully remove the meat, carrots, onions, and leeks from the stock. Set the meat aside to cool, then refrigerate.

[5] Strain the stock and reduce until flavourful and thick. Mix the cornstarch with a little cold water until smooth, then add gradually to the simmering stock until it reaches a rich, glossy consistency. Strain and set aside.

[6] Blend all the Sichuan sauce ingredients until smooth. Stir into the reduced stock spoon by spoon until you reach the desired flavour and texture.

[7] Cut each beef cheek into three pieces. Place in the sauce and warm slowly for 10–15 minutes, basting regularly. The sauce will become shiny and cling to the meat. Watch carefully; it can stick to the bottom of the pan so add a splash of water if needed.

CHEF'S NOTE

I think of this dish as very similar to bœuf bourguignon — but done my way. Ask your butcher to trim the beef cheek of excess fat and sinew, keeping it in one large piece. We usually cook it in the oven at the restaurant, but a large pot or pan works just as well. Also, don't use an overly salted or spicy chilli oil for the Sichuan sauce. I love to serve this dish with freshly cut kumquat and blood orange, skin removed. For a side, steamed eggplant without the skin or spinach seasoned with fresh ginger and sesame oil are both perfect.

Nina Métayer

Founder, Délicatisserie

Quick-Fire Question Round

Sweet or Savoury?

Surf, Turf or Greens?

Pasta or Rice?

Gourmet or Street Eats?

Depends on the day

Baked, Fried or Grilled?

Nina is a French pastry chef who was named World Confectioner 2023 by the International Union of Bakers and Confectioners, and World's Best Pastry Chef 2024 by The World's 50 Best. She launched her online boutique in 2021, followed by four physical shops — two in Paris and two in La Rochelle, her hometown. For Nina, cooking is about sharing and, above all, bringing joy to others. She always cooks more for others than for herself, a generosity she proudly inherited from her mother.

DÉLICATISSERIE Printemps Homme (8th floor), Printemps Haussmann, 64 Boulevard Haussmann, 75009 Paris

delicatisserie.com

p. 187

What is your go-to comfort food and why?
A piece of cheese on bread because the simplest things are the best, but if I don't have cheese, butter is also perfect.

What's a staple ingredient in your fridge?
Butter and fleur de sel.

What do you love about the food scene in your city?
The diversity of the bistros and the creativity of the chefs. Each kitchen has its own identity, and I love it when the chefs embody their cuisine.

What is a dish that everyone should try at least once?
Tartiflette is my favorite dish, along with croziflette. It's a dish for sharing with family and friends, and everyone enjoys it.

What is one thing you wish people understood about your culture's cuisine?
I hope people can see all the love my team and I pour into creating our beautiful pastries — and above all, that they feel the value of the ingredients we carefully source: the fruits, the butter, the flour, and all the others, each grown or prepared by passionate artisans and dedicated professionals.

What is your favourite food-related memory?
My grandparents' stuffed tomatoes... I still remember their smell and taste, as if it were yesterday. My grandfather grew beautiful tomatoes in his garden, and my grandmother canned them before winter. She used them in many dishes, but stuffed tomatoes were undoubtedly my favourite.

Which restaurant in your city should visitors check out at least once?
Baetriz Gonzalez's restaurants and Café de Luce at Montmartre by Amandine Chaignot.

Chocolate Macaron (35)

Ideal for casual afternoon tea or refined gatherings.

Yields 30 pieces

- Icing sugar 330 g
- Almond powder (ground almonds) 210 g
- Cocoa powder 30 g
- Egg whites 180 g
- Granulated sugar 68 g
- Heavy cream 160 g
- Dark chocolate 100 g
- Milk chocolate 50 g
- Praliné 50 g
- Fleur de sel (salt) 1.5 g

[1] **Macaron shells:** Using a piping bag fitted with an 8 mm round tip, pipe small, evenly sized rounds in a staggered pattern on a baking sheet. Let the shells dry for 40 minutes, then bake at 160 °C for 20 minutes.

[2] **Chocolate ganache:** Bring the cream to a boil and pour over the chopped chocolate. Mix and blend until smooth. Add the praline and fleur de sel, mix again. Refrigerate for 45 minutes to set.

[3] **To assemble:** Soften the ganache with a spatula, then transfer to a piping bag fitted with an 8 mm round tip. Pipe ganache onto half the shells and sandwich with the remaining shells of matching size.

CHEF'S NOTE

I often make this recipe with my daughters — especially this chocolate version, which I love and is always a hit with the kids. It's also the kind of treat you can make a little too much of; it keeps really well.

Flan Tonka (36)

Perfect for occasions that call for warmth and subtle indulgence.

Serves 6 pax

– Softened butter	150 g
– Icing sugar	90 g
– Almond powder	30 g
– Salt	2.5 g
– Ground vanilla	1 g
– All-purpose flour (T55)	270 g
– Egg	1
– Whole milk	450 g
– Heavy cream	130 g
– Tonka bean	1/2
– Granulated sugar	79 g
– Egg yolks	65 g
– Cornstarch	39 g
– Butter	65 g

Sweet pastry dough:

[1] Using either your hands or a stand mixer with the paddle attachment, rub the butter, icing sugar, almond powder, salt, ground vanilla, and flour. Add the egg and mix until the dough is smooth and homogeneous. Wrap in plastic wrap and refrigerate for 2 hours.

[2] Butter a tart ring 18 cm in diameter and 6 cm high. Roll out the dough to 3 mm thickness. Cut out a circle 18 cm in diameter for the base, and a strip 6 cm wide for the sides. Line the tart ring with the dough and freeze for 30 minutes.

Flan custard filling:

[3] In a saucepan, bring the milk, cream, and grated tonka bean to a boil. In a separate bowl, whisk together the sugar and egg yolks until pale, then add the cornstarch. Gradually pour the hot milk and cream mixture over the egg mixture while whisking, then return everything to the saucepan. Cook over low heat, whisking constantly. Continue cooking for 1 minute after it comes to a boil. Remove from the heat and add the butter, cut into small pieces.

[4] Pour the pastry cream into the sweet pastry shell straight from the freezer.

[5] Freeze the assembled flan for 1 hour.

[6] Bake for 45 minutes at 180 °C (356 °F).

[7] Unmould immediately after baking and let cool to room temperature in the ring. Once cooled, remove the ring and refrigerate the flan for 2 hours.

CHEF'S NOTE

Take your time to cook it and give it time to cool.

Omar Dhiab

Chef-owner, Restaurant Omar Dhiab & Elbi

Omar is a French chef who grew up cooking with his father, a professional cook, learning family recipes like poultry with jute mallow leaves and Sunday lamb with orzo. After training at Le Train Bleu, Pavillon Ledoyen, and under Christophe Moret at Lasserre and L'Abeille at the Shangri-La, he opened his eponymous restaurant in Paris's 1st arrondissement in 2022, earning a Michelin star six months later. His generous, modern cuisine is built around deeply flavoured sauces and seasonings—both animal and plant-based—that unite childhood memories with meticulous technique.

RESTAURANT OMAR DHIAB — 23 Rue Hérold, 75001 Paris — omardhiab.com

ELBI — 54 Rue de Paradis, 75010 Paris — restaurantelbi.fr

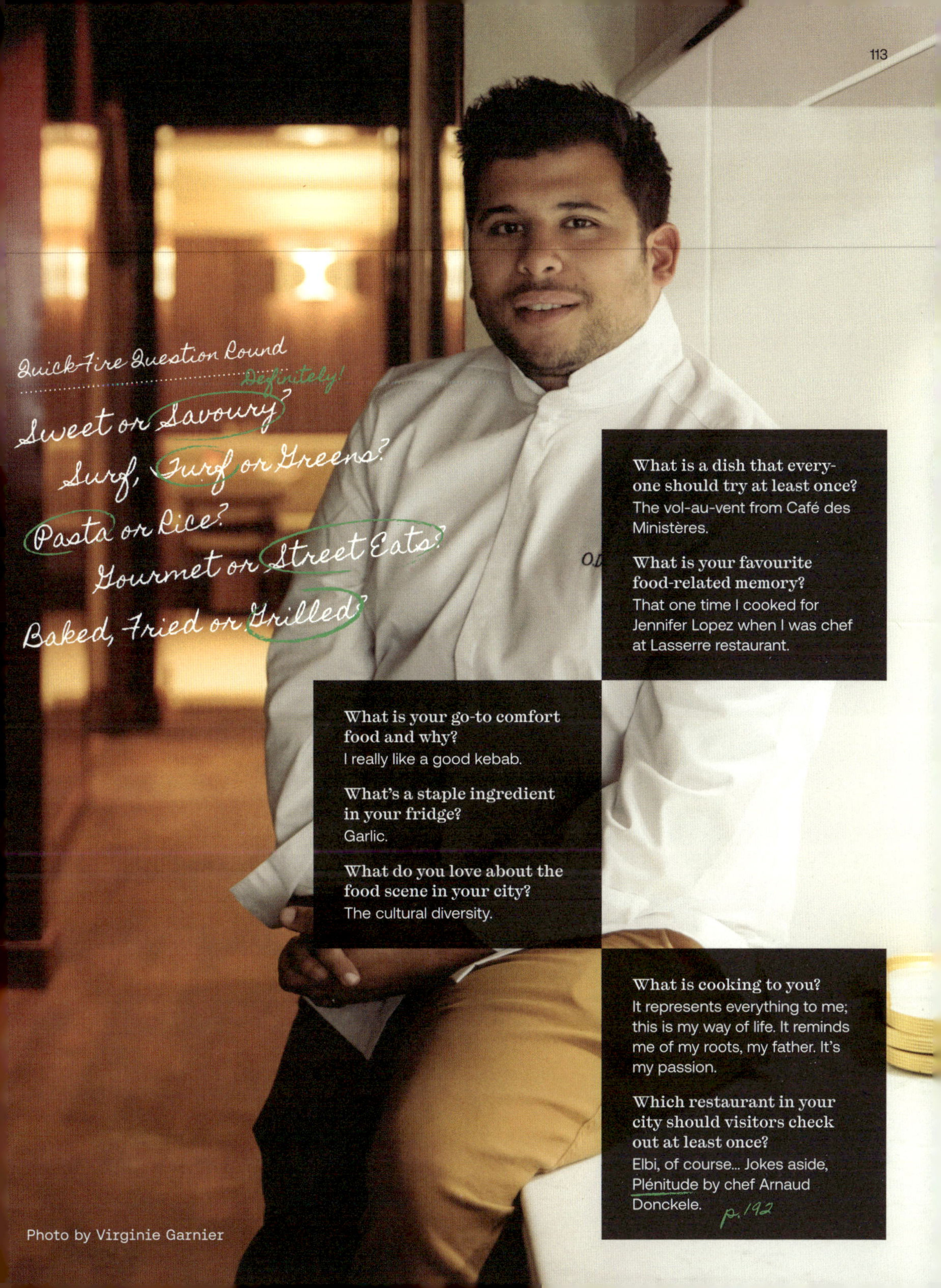

Quick-Fire Question Round

Sweet or Savoury? Definitely!

Surf, Turf or Greens?

Pasta or Rice?

Gourmet or Street Eats?

Baked, Fried or Grilled?

What is a dish that everyone should try at least once?
The vol-au-vent from Café des Ministères.

What is your favourite food-related memory?
That one time I cooked for Jennifer Lopez when I was chef at Lasserre restaurant.

What is your go-to comfort food and why?
I really like a good kebab.

What's a staple ingredient in your fridge?
Garlic.

What do you love about the food scene in your city?
The cultural diversity.

What is cooking to you?
It represents everything to me; this is my way of life. It reminds me of my roots, my father. It's my passion.

Which restaurant in your city should visitors check out at least once?
Elbi, of course... Jokes aside, Plénitude by chef Arnaud Donckele. p.192

Photo by Virginie Garnier

Veal Sweetbread Croque with Grenobloise Condiment & Veal Jus (37)

Where classic French technique meets unapologetic indulgence.

– Veal sweetbreads	1 kg
– Veal rump	300 g
– Double cream	100 ml
– Egg whites	50 g
– White sandwich loaf	1
– Unwaxed lemons	300 g
– Sugar	50 g
– Capers	1 tbsp
– Marjoram	1/4 bunch
– Chervil	1/4 bunch
– Extra virgin olive oil	50 ml
– Veal breast	2 kg
– Shallots	2
– Sarawak pepper	10 g
– Garlic cloves	2
– Marjoram sprigs	2

[1] **Sweetbread croque:** Blanch the sweetbreads from a cold water start for 10 minutes. Refresh in iced water, peel, and cut into 1 cm dice. Roast in butter until golden. Cool quickly. Blend the veal rump with the cream and egg whites, then pass through a fine sieve until smooth. Fold in the roasted sweetbread dice. Line a 15×15 cm frame with crustless sliced bread. Fill with the mixture and top with another layer of bread. Cover with cling film and steam at 80 °C for 40 minutes. Once cooled, slice and toast in a pan with olive oil for 2 minutes per side.

[2] **Grenobloise condiment:** Segment the lemons and cut into large quarters. Place in a saucepan with the sugar and cook very gently until lightly candied. Once cooled, emulsify with the olive oil. Add the capers and finely chopped marjoram and chervil.

[3] **Veal jus:** Roast the veal breast in oil and butter. Cover with chicken stock and cook for 1 hour. Infuse with marjoram at the last moment.

[4] **To serve:** Spoon the grenobloise condiment onto the plate, place a spinach leaf on top with the sweetbread croque alongside. Serve the veal jus in a small jug.

Pham Cyril-Tuan

Sous-chef, Hanada

Cyril-Tuan grew up in Brittany, where his childhood was shaped by Vietnamese flavours passed down through his family. Over 12 years in Paris kitchens—including Guilo Guilo, Dersou and Ogata—he absorbed Japanese techniques and French tradition, weaving all three influences into his cooking. Now sous-chef at the omakase restaurant Hanada, he brings together the precision of Japan, the warmth of Vietnam, and the foundation of French cuisine in every dish.

Quick-Fire Question Round

Sweet or Savoury? Always!
Surf, Turf or Greens?
Pasta or Rice?
Gourmet or Street Eats?
Baked, Fried or Grilled?

What is your favourite food-related memory?
One of my earliest food memories is eating whatever I wanted in the kitchen of my family's restaurant as a kid.

Which restaurant in your city should visitors check out at least once? p. 182
In Paris, I'd recommend La Biche au Bois. Opened in 1929, this intimate restaurant serves timeless French classics and remains one of my favourite hidden gems.

What is your go-to comfort food and why?
I always go for a phở — in any season, it just makes you feel good.

What do you love about the food scene in your city?
The quality of ingredients is really good.

What is a dish that everyone should try at least once?
Andouillette and French fries.

Mackerel & Nuoc Mam with Rice Powder (38)

Where ocean richness meets bright, savoury intensity.

– Fresh mackerel fillets, Pinboned	2
– Rice vinegar	2 tbsp
– Sugar	1 tbsp
– Salt	1 tsp
– Nuoc mam (Vietnamese fish sauce)	2 tbsp
– Water	1 tbsp
– Sugar	1 tbsp
– Garlic clove, finely minced	1
– Lime juice	1 tsp
– Small red chilli, finely sliced (optional)	1
– Roasted rice powder	1 tbsp

[1] **Mackerel or shime saba:** Dissolve the sugar and salt in rice vinegar. Pour over the mackerel fillets and marinate in the fridge for 4–6 hours until firm.

[2] **Nuoc mam sauce:** Mix the nuoc mam, water, sugar, garlic, lime juice, and chilli until the sugar dissolves. Adjust seasoning to taste.

[3] **Roasted rice powder:** Toast uncooked sticky rice in a dry pan over medium heat, stirring constantly, until golden and fragrant. Cool, then grind to a fine powder.

[4] **To serve:** Remove the mackerel from the marinade and pat dry. Place on a serving plate, drizzle with the nuoc mam sauce, and finish with a generous sprinkle of roasted rice powder.

CHEF'S NOTE

This simple dish, packed with bold flavours, is the first recipe I've ever created — a mix of Japanese techniques and Vietnamese flavours. I prepped the fish as they do in Japan but seasoned it like they do back home. Garnish with fresh herbs such as coriander or rau răm for freshness.

Smoky Mezcal Mascarpone with Rosemary Milk Jelly & Blood Orange (39)

Perfect for ending dinners on a bold, aromatic note.

– Mascarpone cheese	250 g
– Mezcal	50 ml
– Whole milk	300 ml
– Fresh rosemary sprigs	2
– Gelatin sheets (or powdered gelatin)	3 g
– Sugar	2 tbsp
– Blood orange, peeled and segmented	1

Rosemary-infused milk jelly veil:

[1] Heat milk gently with rosemary sprigs until just simmering. Remove from heat and let infuse for 15 minutes. Strain out the rosemary.

[2] Return milk to gentle heat, add agar-agar powder, whisk well, and bring to a boil for 1-2 minutes to activate agar.

[3] Pour the milk mixture very thinly onto a flat tray or silicone mat to form a thin "veil" layer. Let cool until set (about 1 hour).

Mascarpone cream:

[4] Whisk mascarpone with mezcal and sugar until smooth and creamy.

To serve:

[5] Spoon mascarpone cream onto serving plates or glasses.

[6] Arrange blood orange segments directly on top of the mascarpone.

[7] Carefully place the milk jelly veil over the orange and cream, covering them gently.

CHEF'S NOTE

Add pollen on the top for a subtle floral and slightly sweet taste.

Pierre-Antoine Darsy

Chef-owner, Bistrot Darsy

Quick-Fire Question Round

Sweet or Savoury?

Surf, Turf or Greens?

Pasta or Rice?

Gourmet or Street Eats? Both :p

Baked, Fried or Grilled?

Pierre-Antoine opened Bistrot Darsy in the heart of Ménilmontant to serve the generous, comforting food of his childhood—roast chicken, boeuf bourguignon, eggs with mayonnaise—in a neighbourhood bistro where people eat well and return often. He pairs each dish with carefully chosen wines, creating a simple, friendly place built on warmth and flavour. His cooking is rooted in tradition and designed to feel like home.

15 Rue des Panoyaux, 75020 Paris bistrotdarsy.fr

What is your go-to comfort food and why?
A delicious ribeye steak with homemade chips and a blue cheese or mushroom sauce.

What's a staple ingredient in your fridge?
Pickles, jam and cheese. I could make meals just with those and by combining them.

What do you love about the food scene in your city?
Paris is a fantastic city when it comes to the gastronomic scene; you can find everything and anything.

What is your favourite food-related memory?
Sunday meals with friends, lasting from noon until evening. Or we finish dessert around 5 p.m. and move on to aperitifs around 6 p.m. Enjoying a delicious roast chicken and melt-in-the-mouth potatoes.

What is cooking to you?
To me, cooking is all about "creating an event" and sharing emotions. Whether it's for my friends, my family, or my customers, I love the idea of a dish becoming a rendezvous point. I enjoy the way food brings people together – like that feeling when you say, "It's moules-frites at my place this weekend!" That sense of conviviality and the anticipation of a shared meal are what truly drive me.

Which restaurant in your city should visitors check out at least once?
Au Moulin à Vent in the 5th arrondissement of Paris, one of my favourite bistros.

Bœuf Bourguignon (40)

A timeless expression of French countryside cooking.

Serves 4–6 pax

– Stewing beef – chuck, neck or shank (short ribs or cheek also work well)	2-3 kg
– Smoked pork belly	1-2 kg
– Red wine	
– Onions	3
– Garlic	
– Carrots	2
– A little celery	
– 1 bouquet garni (parsley, thyme, bay leaf)	
– Salt	
– Pepper	
– Butter	
– A little flour	

[1] Cut the beef and smoked pork belly into 4–6 cm pieces.

[2] Melt the butter and fry the onions, carrots, and celery until the onions begin to turn translucent, then set aside.

[3] Over a high heat, brown the meat well on all sides. Sprinkle with flour and cook a little longer.

[4] Lower the heat, then return the onions, carrots, and celery to the pan.

[5] Pour in the wine and add the bouquet garni. Cover and simmer over a low heat for at least 4–5 hours, stirring occasionally and adding more wine if needed.

CHEF'S NOTE

This is the first dish my grandmother taught me: my introduction to cooking. It's very simple to make; you just need time and patience. It is a convivial dish, not too expensive to make, and tastes even better prepared over several days. For the best results, marinate the meat the night before in the red wine, onions, garlic, bouquet garni, and carrots, then reuse everything in the stock. Use a cast iron casserole dish if you can. Serve straight from the pot in the middle of the table with potatoes or pasta.

Priscilla Trâm

Chef-owner, Trâm 130

Priscilla is the chef and founder of Trâm 130, which opened in Paris's 11th arrondissement in September 2024. Born to a Vietnamese family steeped in hospitality, she absorbed the rhythm of service from childhood but initially pursued law, practising anti-corruption work in Hong Kong for five years. There, she discovered the city's intimate private kitchens, which ignited her passion for cooking. Back in Paris, she began hosting ephemeral dinners by night while working as a lawyer by day, eventually building a devoted following through pop-ups and residencies. Her precise, balanced bistro cooking is guided by flavour, seasoning, and umami, blending French technique with Southeast Asian influences, and the bold, clean spirit of San Sebastián.

Quick-Fire Question Round

Sweet or Savoury?

Surf, Turf or Greens?

Pasta or Rice? Neither

Gourmet or Street Eats? ....that taste gourmet

Baked, Fried or Grilled? Ideally over charcoal

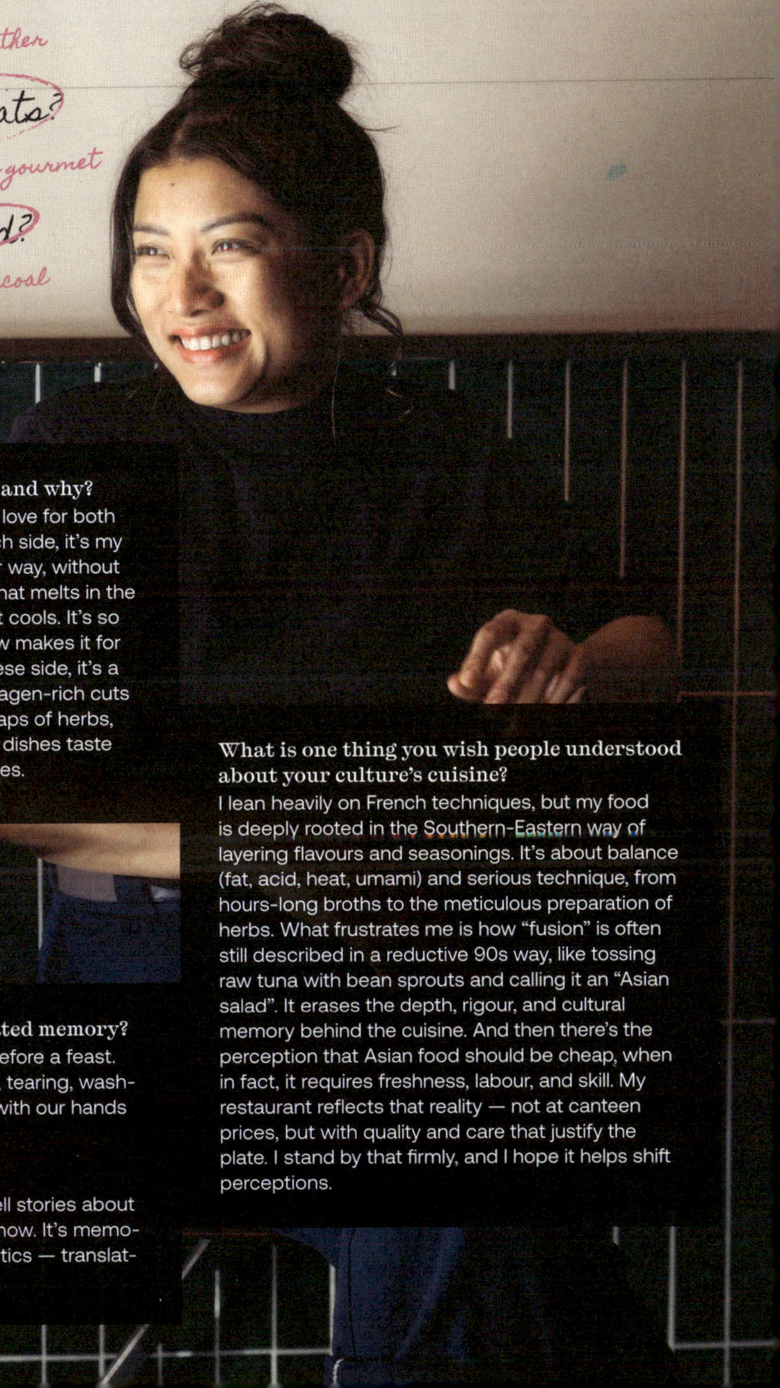

What is your go-to comfort food and why?
My comfort food reflects my double love for both of my cultural worlds. From my French side, it's my mom's endives au jambon — but her way, without béchamel. She uses crème fraîche that melts in the oven and then gently sets again as it cools. It's so comforting that even my partner now makes it for me on rainy days. From my Vietnamese side, it's a steaming bowl of pho with fatty, collagen-rich cuts of meat, a deeply troubled broth, heaps of herbs, and always extra lime and chili. Both dishes taste like home to me, in different languages.

What is your favourite food-related memory?
Making herb plates with my family before a feast. Everyone gathered around the table, tearing, washing, and chatting. The meal started with our hands long before it reached the stove.

What is cooking to you?
Cooking is my language. It's how I tell stories about where I come from and where I am now. It's memory, identity, and sometimes even politics — translated into something you can taste.

What is one thing you wish people understood about your culture's cuisine?
I lean heavily on French techniques, but my food is deeply rooted in the Southern-Eastern way of layering flavours and seasonings. It's about balance (fat, acid, heat, umami) and serious technique, from hours-long broths to the meticulous preparation of herbs. What frustrates me is how "fusion" is often still described in a reductive 90s way, like tossing raw tuna with bean sprouts and calling it an "Asian salad". It erases the depth, rigour, and cultural memory behind the cuisine. And then there's the perception that Asian food should be cheap, when in fact, it requires freshness, labour, and skill. My restaurant reflects that reality — not at canteen prices, but with quality and care that justify the plate. I stand by that firmly, and I hope it helps shift perceptions.

Signature Beef Tartare with Herbs on a Roasted Bone Marrow (41)

Where rustic decadence meets refined precision.

– Centre-cut beef marrow bone, ~20 cm long, split lengthwise	1
– Sea salt	
– Neutral oil for brushing	
– Beef tenderloin or sirloin, finely chopped	80 g
– Fish sauce	1 tsp
– Lime juice	1 tsp
– Palm sugar or white sugar	1/8 tsp
– Toasted rice powder	1/2 tsp
– Shallot, finely chopped	1 tsp
– Garlic, finely chopped	1 tsp
– Fresh chilli, finely chopped (optional)	1/2 tsp
– Fresh coriander, mint, or Thai basil, finely chopped (optional)	1 tsp
– Crisp bread (grilled baguette or soudough)	
– Pickled mustard seeds	1/2 tsp

[1] **Bone marrow:** Preheat the oven to 220 °C. Place the marrow bone cut-side up on a tray, brush lightly with oil, and season with sea salt. Roast for 15–20 minutes until the marrow is bubbling and just starting to pull away from the bone, but not melted out. Keep warm.

[2] **Tartare:** In a chilled bowl, dissolve the sugar in the fish sauce and lime juice. Add the beef, shallot, garlic, toasted rice powder, chilli, and herbs. Mix gently. Adjust seasoning accordingly — more lime for freshness, a splash of water if too salty.

[3] **To serve:** Spoon the tartare neatly over the roasted bone marrow. Garnish with pickled mustard seeds and serve immediately with toasted or grilled bread for scooping.

CHEF'S NOTE

The marrow bone acts as both vessel and flavour — smoky, rich marrow supporting a bright, acidic, and nutty tartare.

Robert Mendoza

Chef

Robert is a Paris-based chef who blends his Mexican heritage with modern European techniques. Having worked at Verjus, Hertog Jan, and The Willows Inn, he developed a style defined by aesthetic precision and bold flavour, earning recognition at Le Saint Sébastien before leading Vivant 2 as one of Paris's most exciting culinary voices. For Robert, cooking is storytelling — a way to preserve memory, culture, and emotion on a plate. Both deeply personal and profoundly communal, his cuisine unites technique and instinct, history and invention — love made tangible.

@RAWBGOLD

Quick-Fire Question Round

Sweet or Savoury?

Surf, Turf or Greens?

Pasta or Rice?

Gourmet or Street Eats? Both!

Baked, Fried or Grilled?

What is your go-to comfort food and why?
Tacos! They are the perfect food!

What's a staple ingredient in your fridge?
We always have chilli oil on hand.

What do you love about the food scene in your city?
I love that you can choose to eat at a very fine dining restaurant or have crêpes on the street.

What is a dish that everyone should try at least once?
A classic Mexican street sandwich called pambazos.

What is one thing you wish people understood about your culture's cuisine?
Mexican cuisine is one of the world's oldest culinary traditions — rich in history, culture, and ancestral techniques.

What is your favourite food-related memory?
Some of my earliest and most cherished memories are of helping my grandmother in the kitchen. I'd stand beside her, mesmerised as she chopped, mixed, and seasoned with such love and care. To me, it wasn't just cooking — it was magic, and she was the magician.

Which restaurant in your city should visitors check out at least once?
Cheval d'or.

p. 179

Tuna Carpaccio with Salsa Macha (42)

Ideal for sophisticated cocktail evenings and curated small plates.

- Bluefin tuna steaks (120 g each) — 2
- Chile Guajillo, deseeded — 50 g
- Shallot, chopped — 1
- Garlic clove — 1
- Peanuts, toasted & chopped — 30 g
- Sesame seeds — 1 tsp
- Sherry vinegar — 20 ml
- Grapeseed oil — 150 ml
- Kewpie mayonnaise — 20 g
- Pickles
- Salt
- Pepper

[1] **Salsa macha:** Heat the grapeseed oil in a saucepan to 180°C. Add the guajillos, garlic, and shallots. Cook for 2–3 minutes until lightly browned. Leave to cool, then blend with a pinch of salt and pepper until smooth. Transfer to a bowl and stir in the peanuts, sesame seeds, and sherry vinegar. Adjust seasoning and set aside.

[2] **Tuna:** Lay a sheet of baking paper on a board. Place one tuna steak on top and cover with another sheet. Gently pound with a rolling pin until evenly thinned out. Repeat with the second steak.

[3] **To serve:** Spread 10 g of Kewpie mayonnaise on each plate and lay the tuna on top to cover. Dress with the salsa macha, finish with your favourite pickles and fresh herbs.

CHEF'S NOTE

This recipe captures the essence of how I cook — rooted in Mexican tradition but expressed through a contemporary lens. The tuna carpaccio brings freshness and precision, while the salsa macha brings depth and emotion — a nod to my heritage, my family, and the bold flavours I grew up with. A few flakes of sea salt or a splash of lime juice right before serving will brighten the whole dish.

Rodrigue Barcilon

Chef-owner, OTÉ

Rodrigue is the chef behind OTÉ, a Paris restaurant that brings the intense, flavourful cuisine of Réunion to life. His cooking blends the island's classic dishes with the vibrant energy of street food, inviting diners on a journey through bold spices, Creole traditions, and the spirit of the island.

46 Rue Jean-Pierre Timbaud, 75011 Paris · ote-restaurant.com

Quick-Fire Question Round

Sweet or Savoury?

Surf, Turf or Greens?

Pasta or Rice? It's like asking me 'mum or dad'!

Gourmet or Street Eats?

Baked, Fried or Grilled?

What is your go-to comfort food and why?
A rougail saucisses, of course!

What's a staple ingredient in your fridge?
Spicy paste.

What do you love about the food scene in your city?
The creativity.

What is one thing you wish people understood about your culture's cuisine?
I love the mix of cultures and cuisines you find in Paris — this blend inspires me every day.

What is a dish that everyone should try at least once?
The famous bouchons of the Réunion.

What is your favourite food-related memory?
A tapa de pulpo in Seville. It's the kind of dish that's simple but unforgettable: tender octopus, a drizzle of olive oil, maybe a sprinkle of paprika, and that perfect Andalusian atmosphere.

What is cooking to you?
Relaxation and creativity.

Which restaurant in your city should visitors check out at least once?
OTÉ, of course!

Photo by The Travel Buds

Rougail Saucisses (43)

Perfect for lively gatherings filled with warmth and spice.

Serves 4 pax

– Montbéliard sausages	650 g
– Tomatoes, fresh or tinned	600 g
– Red onion	150 g
– Garlic	20 g
– Ginger	12 g
– Red chilli pepper	8 g
– Turmeric	5 g
– Pepper	1/2 tsp
– Sugar	1/2 tsp
– Vegetable oil	150 ml
– Salt	
– Pepper	

[1] Slice the red onions into thin strips. Peel and finely chop the ginger, garlic, and chilli. Cut the sausages into 1 cm slices.

[2] Heat the oil in a large pot over high heat until shimmering. Add the ginger, chilli, and garlic and sauté for about 5 minutes.

[3] Add the sausages and brown for a few minutes, then add the red onions and stir in the turmeric. Cook over medium heat for about 15 minutes, stirring regularly.

[4] Add the tomatoes and season with sugar, salt, and pepper. Simmer over low to medium heat for 1 hour 30 minutes until the sauce thickens nicely.

CHEF'S NOTE

This is a convivial, comforting dish to share with friends or family. Serve with white basmati rice and green lentils seasoned with massalé. For extra crunch, add crispy fried onions — and for the adventurous, a small spoonful of chilli paste. A cucumber relish (rougail concombre) on the side brings freshness and a zesty kick.

Potatoe Cookie (44)

For a delicious break in the afternoon.

Yields 10 cookies

– Salted butter	260 g
– White sugar	120 g
– Brown sugar	100 g
– Flour	200 g
– Cornstarch	100 g
– Eggs	2
– Dark chocolate (70%)	240 g
– Sweet potatoes	200 g

Before you start:

[1] Take the butter out of the fridge 1 to 2 hours in advance so it can soften to a creamy texture. Cut it into small cubes. Peel the sweet potatoes and cut them into cubes. In a saucepan, cook the sweet potatoes in water for about 30 minutes, starting with cold water. Once cooked, drain and let cool, then mash them with a fork (not too finely) so there are still small chunks of sweet potato in the cookies.

In a large mixing bowl:

[2] Mix the two types of sugar (white and brown) and add the softened butter. Beat together until smooth and creamy.

[3] Add the eggs and mix again.

[4] Add the flour and cornstarch, then mix once more.

[5] Add the mashed sweet potato and mix again. Add the dark chocolate and stir to combine — this is your final dough.

[6] Cover the bowl with plastic wrap, label it, and refrigerate for about 1 to 3 hours to let the dough firm up. Form spherical dough balls of about 110 g each.

CHEF'S NOTE

Add some fleur de sel on top!

La Patate Lé La (45)

A celebration of the humble potato, reimagined with flair.

Serves 4 pax

– Sweet potatoes	2
– Massalé spice mix	30 g
– Vegetable oil	30 g
– Garlic	15 g
– Ginger	15 g
– Red chili pepper	15 g
– Coconut cream	0.5 L
– Turmeric	10 g
– Soy sauce	10 g
– Peanut paste (such as Dakatine)	30 g
– Crushed peanuts	30 g
– Chives, bunch	1
– Cucumber	1
– Lime	1
– Hot sauce (sriracha)	
– Garlic	10 g
– Ginger	10 g
– Red chili pepper	10 g
– Fresh kaffir lime (combava)	1

[1] **Sweet potatoes:** Cut the sweet potatoes in half lengthwise and trim the ends so they sit flat in the baking dish. Score the flesh with a knife in a 0.5 cm grid pattern. Mix the vegetable oil and massalé, then brush generously over the sweet potatoes. Bake at 170 °C (340 °F) for at least 45 minutes. Check doneness by piercing the sweet potatoes with a skewer or knife when they come out of the oven.

[2] **Coconut-turmeric-peanut sauce:** In a saucepan, add a splash of vegetable oil, then finely chop and sauté the garlic, ginger, and chili over medium heat for about 3 minutes. Add the coconut cream, soy sauce, turmeric, and peanut paste. Whisk vigorously to combine everything evenly. Simmer over medium heat for 15 minutes. Strain the sauce using a fine-mesh sieve (chinois) into a container.

[3] **Condiments & cucumber rougail:** Cut the cucumber into 1 cm pieces, then pulse in a food processor to chop fi ner. Add garlic, ginger, chili, juice of half a lime, and season with salt and pepper. Crush some peanuts and finely chop the chives.

[4] **To serve:** Heat the coconut–turmeric–peanut sauce. Reheat the sweet potatoes in the oven. Spread the cucumber condiment along the length of each sweet potato. Add small dollops of hot sauce, then sprinkle with crushed peanuts and chives. Pour a ladle of sauce into a shallow bowl, carefully place the sweet potato on top, and finish by zesting the kaffir lime (combava) over the dish.

Ryuichi Utsumi

Chef, erh

Ryuichi began his career in the sushi world in his native Osaka before deciding to broaden his horizons by learning French gastronomy and moving to Paris. Drawing on his deep knowledge of Japanese cuisine and newfound mastery of French techniques, he creates a unique style that transports diners between France and Japan with every dish.

11 Rue Tiquetonne, 75002 Paris · restaurant-erh.com

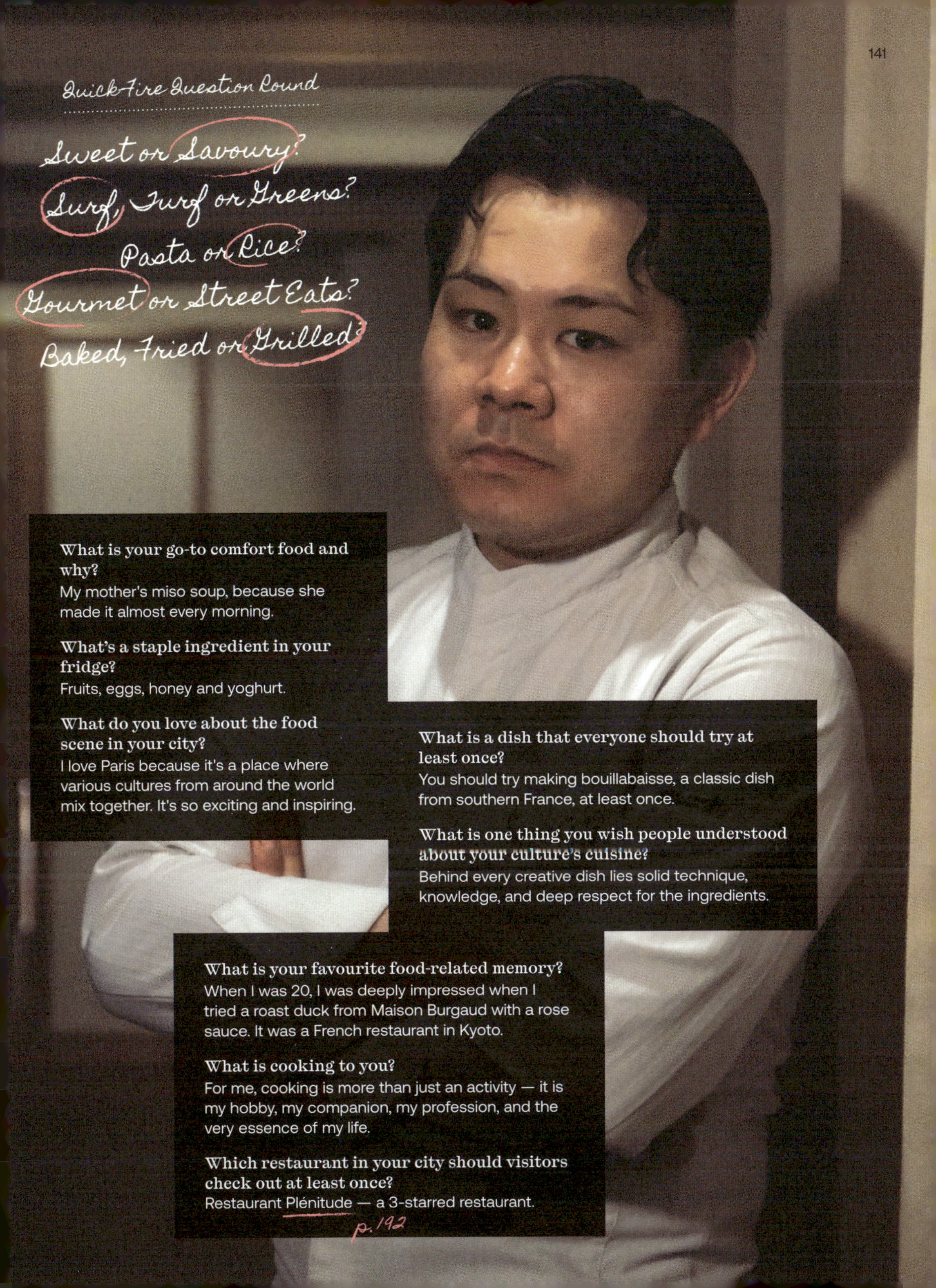

Quick-Fire Question Round

Sweet or **Savoury**?

Surf, Turf or Greens?

Pasta or **Rice**?

Gourmet or Street Eats?

Baked, Fried or **Grilled**?

What is your go-to comfort food and why?
My mother's miso soup, because she made it almost every morning.

What's a staple ingredient in your fridge?
Fruits, eggs, honey and yoghurt.

What do you love about the food scene in your city?
I love Paris because it's a place where various cultures from around the world mix together. It's so exciting and inspiring.

What is a dish that everyone should try at least once?
You should try making bouillabaisse, a classic dish from southern France, at least once.

What is one thing you wish people understood about your culture's cuisine?
Behind every creative dish lies solid technique, knowledge, and deep respect for the ingredients.

What is your favourite food-related memory?
When I was 20, I was deeply impressed when I tried a roast duck from Maison Burgaud with a rose sauce. It was a French restaurant in Kyoto.

What is cooking to you?
For me, cooking is more than just an activity — it is my hobby, my companion, my profession, and the very essence of my life.

Which restaurant in your city should visitors check out at least once?
Restaurant Plénitude — a 3-starred restaurant.

p.192

Meunière of Turbot with Seasonal Vegetables & Leek Miso (46)

A classic meunière reimagined with subtle umami depth.

– Turbot	200 g
– Butter	50 g
– Flour	10 g
– Chives	100 g
– Grapeseed oil	100 g
– Green courgette, diced into 1 cm pieces	100 g
– Shallot, finely chopped	30 g
– Garlic, finely chopped	10 g
– Green onion miso paste	30 g
– Swiss chard	1
– Spring onions	2
– Potatoes	60 g
– Sugar snap peas	4
– Butter	15 g
– Extra virgin olive oil	10 g
– Chicken bouillon	150 g
– Almonds	4
– Dill	1 bunch
– Lemon marigold	1 bunch

[1] **Courgette & miso:** Heat a drizzle of olive oil in a frying pan and sauté the courgette over medium heat until nicely browned. Add the shallots and garlic, lower the heat, and cook briefly. Stir in the green onion miso and set aside.

[2] **Chive oil & turbot:** Blend the chives with grapeseed oil, then strain to obtain a smooth chive oil. Cook the turbot meunière-style in butter, keeping the temperature gentle to avoid overcooking.

[3] **Vegetables:** Melt butter with a little olive oil, chicken bouillon, and a pinch of salt. Add the spring onion, Swiss chard stems, and pre-fried potatoes. Cook for about 2 minutes. Add the Swiss chard leaves and sugar snap peas, cooking briefly until just tender.

[4] **To serve:** Arrange the potatoes and Swiss chard leaves on the base of the plate. Place the turbot on top, followed by the sautéed vegetables. Garnish with tagetes flowers, fresh herbs, and almonds. Finish with a drizzle of chive oil.

CHEF'S NOTE

I use miso from my hometown and French turbot to create a light, refreshing dish perfect for summer. If turbot is not available, flatfish or John Dory also pair very well. For the full Japanese experience, serve with a glass of Hakugyokuko saké.

Sahra Tallaa

Chef & culinary storyteller

Quick-Fire Question Round

Sweet or Savoury?

Surf, Turf or Greens?

Pasta or Rice?

Gourmet or Street Eats?

Baked, Fried or Grilled?

Sahra is a chef and culinary storyteller who cooks the way one writes — to speak of life, emotions, and memories. Above all, she cooks to make people happy. For her, cooking is emotion before technique — a universal language that can awaken memory, create connection, or comfort someone you love. Nourished by the Mediterranean and shaped by Paris, she creates honest, joyful cuisine where butter meets orange blossom and recipes become fragments of stories. She is fascinated by how one extra ingredient or a missing spice can transform the memory of a dish and turn food into connection.

What is a dish that everyone should try at least once?
Oeuf cocotte with Saint-Marcellin cheese cream, buttered baguette soldiers, and a touch of chives. It's simple and comforting, yet so deeply French — warm, velvety, and just indulgent enough to make you close your eyes with the first spoonful.

What is your favourite food-related memory?
My father's vinaigrette. He'd whisk it directly in the salad bowl, without measuring, just by instinct — a bit of mustard, too much vinegar, and always a laugh at the end. The smell of garlic and shallots meant dinner was almost ready, and life felt simple again. That moment—the clinking fork, the sound of bread tearing, the first bite—that's where my love for cooking was born.

Which restaurant in your city should visitors check out at least once?
Alan Geaam in Paris (16th). It's a place that embodies everything I love about today's French gastronomy: its openness, its generosity, and its deep respect for both ingredients and roots.

What is your go-to comfort food and why?
Fondant de bœuf with caramelised pearl onions and creamy gratin dauphinois. It's the dish that comforts me the most — slow, generous, and deeply French. It doesn't try to impress; it just wraps you in warmth. It has that quiet power to bring you back to yourself — to stillness, to care, to that unspoken "I made this for you".

What's a staple ingredient in your fridge?
Butter. Always. It connects everything — even the most chaotic days. It softens dishes the same way it softens moments.

What do you love about the food scene in your city?
Diversity. Paris is a crossroads. Chefs from everywhere come here and reinvent French gastronomy with their memories, their spices, their way of seeing the world. That's what makes Parisian cuisine so vibrant — this alchemy between heritage and modernity, tradition and curiosity.

French Pot-au-Feu with Bone Marrow, Toasted Bread & Pickles (47)

A timeless French classic, rich with history and comfort.

Beef (paleron, chuck or shank - no macreuse)	1.5 kg
Carrots	3
Leeks	3
Potatoes	4
Artichoke heart	1
Onion	1
Cloves	2
Garlic cloves	2
Bouquet garni (thyme, bay leaf, parsley stems)	1
Bone-marrow bones	4
Coarse grey salt	
Fleur de sel	
Freshly ground black pepper	
Rustic country bread	
Dijon mustard	
Pickles	

[1] Char the onion dry, directly in the pot, until deeply browned — almost black on the edges. Stud with the cloves.

[2] Place the beef paleron and shank in the pot, cover generously with cold water, and bring to a gentle simmer.

[3] Skim carefully and often. For a clear broth, lay a sheet of kitchen paper briefly on the surface to absorb the foam, then lift off.

[4] Once the broth is clean, add the charred onion, garlic, bouquet garni, and a generous handful of coarse salt. Simmer gently, uncovered, for 21/2 hours.

[5] After 11/2 hours, add the carrots. Continue cooking for about 45 minutes.

[6] During the last 30 minutes, add the leeks and artichoke heart — they should stay tender but whole.

[7] Cook the potatoes separately in salted water with a ladle of broth for flavour. Adjust seasoning.

[8] Add the marrow bones for the last 20 minutes only — just enough to warm through without breaking apart.

[9] To serve, layer a piece of tender beef in a deep bowl, some vegetables, and two ladles of hot, clear broth. On the side, serve toasted country bread with warm marrow spread on top, sprinkled with fleur de sel. Add a touch of mustard, a spoonful of broth, a bite of beef, and finish with a pickle.

CHEF'S NOTE

This is the kind of dish that teaches patience — slow, humble, and deeply generous. It's also France in a bowl: honest ingredients, time, and care. Every step has meaning, and every spoonful feels like home. Don't rush the simmering — that's where the magic happens! And always salt the broth only once it is clear, never before: that's the secret to tender, flavourful meat.

Brioche with Mango & Passion Fruit Caramel (48)

Designed for occasions that call for sweetness and flair.

Ingredient	Quantity
– Large egg	1
– Heavy cream	150 ml
– Passion fruits	2
– Brown sugar (divided: 50 g + 100 g)	150 g
– Unsalted butter (divided: 30 g + 20 g + 10 g optional)	60 g
– Passion fruit coulis or juice	150 ml
– Ripe mango	1
– Scoop of good-quality vanilla ice cream	1
– Hint of vanilla (fresh paste or extract)	

[1] In a large bowl, whisk together the egg and cream. Add the pulp of half a passion fruit. Dip thick slices of brioche in the mixture and let them soak a few seconds.

[2] In a non-stick pan, melt 50 g of brown sugar over medium heat until it just turns amber — not too dark, to avoid bitterness. Add 30 g of butter to stop the cooking, then place the soaked brioche slices in the pan. Let them caramelise 2 minutes on each side, until golden and slightly crisp.

[3] In a saucepan, caramelise the remaining 100 g sugar dry. Pour in the passion fruit coulis (it will bubble), reduce slightly, then add 20 g butter and the rest of the passion fruit pulp.

[4] Plate the brioche with mango slices, half a passion fruit, a scoop of vanilla ice cream, and a drizzle of warm passion caramel.

CHEF'S NOTE

Let the brioche really caramelise in the butter and sugar — that's what gives it the perfect crust. And remember: as soon as your caramel turns amber, add the butter immediately to keep it smooth and balanced.

Artichoke Tart Tatin with Smoked Duck & Foie Gras Sauce (49)

A bold composition of texture, warmth and finesse.

- Medium artichoke hearts (fresh or canned, drained; cut in half lengthwise) — 6
- Duck breast, thinly sliced — 8
- Sheet puff pastry — 1
- Butter — 40 g
- Olive oil — 1 tbsp
- Sugar — 2 tbsp
- Small shallot, finely chopped — 1
- Veal or chicken stock — 100 ml
- Foie gras (raw or semi-cooked) — 50 g
- Heavy cream — 30 ml
- Fresh thyme sprigs
- Salt
- Pepper

[1] Cut the artichoke hearts in halves. In a non-stick pan, melt the butter with the olive oil. Add the sugar and let it caramelize lightly. Place the artichoke halves cut-side down and cook over medium heat for 5–6 minutes, until golden and glossy. Season with salt, pepper, and a touch of thyme.

[2] Assemble the tatin by the caramelised artichokes in a small ovenproof pan or individual moulds. Lay the smoked duck slices over them. Cover with puff pastry, tucking the edges gently inside the pan.

[3] Bake at 190 °C (375 °F) for about 20 minutes, until the pastry is golden and crisp. Let rest 2–3 minutes, then flip carefully onto a plate.

[4] Make the foie gras sauce. In a small saucepan, sweat the shallot in a bit of butter. Deglaze with the stock and reduce by half. Add the foie gras and cream, whisk until smooth and velvety. Season lightly.

[5] To serve, place the warm tatin in the center of the plate. Spoon over a ribbon of foie gras sauce and finish with a few thyme leaves or microgreens.

[6] Add a small salad of arugula or frisée dressed in a light vinaigrette on the side to balance the richness.

CHEF'S NOTE

Don't over-caramelise the sugar — it should stay blond to keep the artichokes soft and delicate. And always flip the tatin while it's still warm, before the caramel sets.

Sugio Yamaguchi

Chef-owner, Wani

Sugio creates unique experiences centred around vegetables, infusions, and coffee. As the founder of NIWA and the contemporary tea salon Wani, he crafts bold cuisine rooted in nature and close collaboration with producers. Through culinary creation and artistic partnerships, his projects explore the delicacy of flavours and the beauty of simple gestures.

WANI p. 178

7 ter Rue Saint-Placide, 75006 Paris   wanitparis.com

Quick-Fire Question Round

Sweet or Savoury?

Surf, Turf or Greens?

Pasta or Rice? Both!

Gourmet or Street Eats?

Baked, Fried or Grilled? Wood fire

What is your go-to comfort food and why?
French fries, but only when the oil is clean!

What's a staple ingredient in your fridge?
Yuzu kosho.

What do you love about the food scene in your city?
The diversity.

What is a dish that everyone should try at least once?
Faux filet from Le Sévero.

What is one thing you wish people understood about your culture's cuisine?
Mottainai.

What is your favourite food-related memory?
Trip to Georgia.

What is cooking to you?
Everyday life.

Which restaurant in your city should visitors check out at least once? p.178
Kodawari Ramen Tsukiji and Le Sévero. p.187

Green Houmous (50)

Made for warm afternoons and effortless hosting.

- Shelled chickpeas
- Garlic clove 1
- Pistachio paste
- Pistachio oil
- Salt
- Pita bread

[1] Cook the shelled chickpeas in salted water with 1 clove of garlic.

[2] Once well cooked, drain and mash with 2 spoonfuls of pistachio paste, a little salt, and a generous amount of pistachio oil.

[3] Serve with hot pita bread.

Chips (51)

Perfect for relaxed gatherings with elevated small bites.

- Potatoes
- Shrimp oil
- Salt
- Freshly ground black pepper

[1] Thinly slice the potatoes. Rinse under cold water to remove excess starch, then drain and dry thoroughly.

[2] Heat the shrimp oil to 130–140 °C. Fry the potato slices until tender and lightly crisp.

[3] Drain and season immediately with salt and freshly ground black pepper.

CHEF'S NOTE

(Top) I made this dish when I discovered fresh chickpeas — planted and harvested myself. It was an unforgettable experience and still gives me pure joy.

Friends (52)

A dish built as much on friendship as on flavour.

- Ripe Sicilian avocado 1
- Extra virgin olive oil
- Almond oil
- Sakura cider vinegar
- Red onion, finely sliced
- Japanese curry spice
- Fresh koji (dékoji)
- Oyster juice

[1] Scoop the ripe flesh of the Sicilian avocado with a spoon and place it in a bowl.

[2] Season with the olive oil from Helio and Antoine, and a few drops of the beautifully scented almond oil discovered thanks to Thomas.

[3] Add a splash of sakura cider vinegar made with Manon and Celine, thanks to Yu. Fold in finely sliced red onion from Erwan.

[4] Enhance with a touch of Japanese curry from Mathilde and Ryoko, fresh "dékoji" from Javier and Laurent, and a spoonful of David and Ingrid's extraordinary oyster juice.

[5] Season to taste, arrange simply and serve.

CHEF'S NOTE

When you cook with ingredients grown by friends and serve them on a plate made by one too, it just feels good — doesn't it?

Taku Mikuriya

Executive Chef, Ojii

Taku is a Japanese chef who began his career in New York, where he worked for five years before moving to Paris. He spent a decade as a chef at Guilo Guilo, then became the executive chef at Ojii. He has also launched Bar Omi, a sushi and wine bar that expands his vision of Japanese cuisine in Paris.

6 Rue Perronet, 75007 Paris ojii.fr

Quick-Fire Question Round

Sweet or Savoury?

Surf, Turf or Greens?

Pasta or Rice? Of course

Gourmet or Street Eats?

Baked, Fried or Grilled?

What is your go-to comfort food and why?
Tuna mayo onigiri — it's easy to eat and satisfying.

What's a staple ingredient in your fridge?
Soya sauce, of course.

What do you love about the food scene in your city?
The diversity of food in Paris. You can find anything from good street food to starred restaurants.

What is a dish that everyone should try at least once?
Ramen.

What is one thing you wish people understood about your culture's cuisine?
Umami tastings.

What is your favourite food-related memory?
Fried chicken with ginger by my mom.

What is cooking to you?
It's my passion and my life; it's what made me who I am.

Which restaurant in your city should visitors check out at least once?
Onii-San.

Akami Toro Strataciella (53)

Perfect for artful gatherings where detail defines the table.

– Toro	50 g
– Akami	50 g
– Stracciatella	50 g
– Wasabi	
– Ponzu jelly	
– Pistachio	
– Garlic chips	
– Olive oil	

[1] Smoke both the toro and akami.

[2] Marinate in soy sauce, sake, and mirin for 5 hours.

[3] Slice the toro and akami into sashimi.

[4] Top with stracciatella, ponzu jelly, and pistachios.

Soba Caviar (54)

A meeting of umami depth and delicate brine.

– Soba	80 g
– Cream sauce (for 4 portions)	1 L
– Soy sauce	100 ml
– Mirin	100 ml
– Dashi powder	10 g
– Shitake mushrooms, thinly sliced	20 g
– Caviar	20 g
– Lime zest	

[1] Place the shitake mushrooms, soy sauce, mirin, and dashi powder in a saucepan. Mix well and bring to a boil over high heat.

[2] Once boiling, reduce to medium heat and simmer for 10 minutes, stirring continuously to prevent burning.

[3] In a separate pan, add approximately 200 ml of the cream sauce. Reheat over medium heat, then add the soba noodles.

[4] Gently mix the soba with the cream sauce until well combined. Do not overcook to preserve the noodles' tenderness. Reduce to low heat (or remove from heat) and fold in half of the caviar, then mix gently.

[5] Plate the soba and finish with the remaining caviar on top before serving.

CHEF'S NOTE

(Top) In our restaurant, we smoke the tuna in-house and marinate it with our house blend. The stracciatella is there to create an unexpected pairing — fatty tuna with something creamy is the perfect combination. Also, presentation is key!

(Bottom) For the perfect touch, finish with a little lime zest — and always add more caviar, of course!

Chicken Teriyaki (55)

Made for evenings that call for warmth and familiarity.

– Chicken thigh, skin on	
– Maizena	
– Cream	20 ml
– Dashi stock	200 ml
– Spinach	
– Herbs (coriander, dill)	
– Salsifis	
– Shitake mushrooms	
– Sansho powder	

Teriyaki sauce

– Soy sauce	600 ml
– Sake	600 ml
– Mirin	600 ml
– Vinegar	60 ml
– Sugar	400 g

[1] **Teriyaki sauce:** Place all ingredients in a medium saucepan. Bring to a boil, then reduce to medium heat and simmer for 40 minutes, stirring occasionally. Remove from heat, allow to cool, and set aside until ready to use.

[2] **Dashi cream base:** Dashi cream base: In a saucepan, combine the dashi, cream, shiitake mushrooms, and salsify. Gently simmer until the salsify and mushrooms are tender. Set aside.

[3] **Chicken:** Season the chicken thighs with salt, then lightly coat with maizena (cornstarch). Heat a pan over high heat until hot. Add cold oil, then place the chicken thighs skin-side down. Sear until golden brown, then turn and brown the other side. Transfer to a preheated oven at 220 °C and cook for 6 minutes, ensuring the chicken is cooked through while remaining juicy.

[4] **Vegetables:** Bring the dashi and mushroom mixture back to a boil. Add the spinach and herbs, stirring gently until just tender. Do not overcook. Strain, reserving only the vegetables.

[5] **To serve:** Warm the teriyaki sauce until slightly thickened and glossy. Remove the chicken from the oven, slice into bite-sized pieces and lightly sprinkle with sansho pepper. Plate with the vegetables and finish with the teriyaki sauce.

CHEF'S NOTE

Cook a very good bowl of rice to mix with the sauce!

Toms Berzins

Chef, Le Grand Bain

Quick-Fire Question Round

Sweet or Savoury?

Surf, Turf or Greens?

Pasta or Rice?

Gourmet or Street Eats?

Baked, Fried or Grilled?

Toms is a bold, punk-inspired Latvian chef currently cooking at Le Grand Bain in Paris's 20th arrondissement. Trained in restaurants across Berlin, Reykjavik, Stockholm, and his hometown of Riga, he chose the city as his home, where he blends Nordic flavours with the energy of Parisian food scene. Having worked in Michelin-starred kitchens, he now proudly represents the neo-bistro movement, championing a new generation of chefs committed to breaking away from toxicity in the restaurant industry.

LE GRAND BAIN p. 179 14 Rue Denoyez, 75020 Paris legrandbainparis.com

What's a staple ingredient in your fridge?
I love using zest of bergamote on almost everything. Another staple is sherry vinegar and black garlic.

What do you love about the food scene in your city?
That every day of the month I am able to eat a different cuisine.

What is a dish that everyone should try at least once?
Sticky date pudding with butterscotch sauce in St. John in London.

What is one thing you wish people understood about your culture's cuisine?
Fermented products are good for you!

Which restaurant in your city should visitors check out at least once?
My favourite restaurant in Paris is Cafe du Coin, where the pizzettes and small plates to share are always on point. Consider going to Cendrillon, Le Maquis and Le Rigmarole.

Green Asparagus in Tempura, Roscoff Onion Marmalade & Smoked Sabayon (56)

A beautiful addition to celebratory dinners with a modern edge.

Serves 2–3 pax

- Thin green asparagus — 300 g
- Roscoff onions or shallots — 8
- Caster sugar — 200 g
- Sherry vinegar — 200 ml
- Olive oil — 50 ml
- Egg yolks — 250 g
- Sunflower oil — 500 ml
- Hay — 50 g
- T65 flour — 200 g
- Cornstarch — 70 g
- IPA beer — 300 ml
- Sparkling water — 150 ml
- Neutral oil for deep frying — 1 L
- Salt
- Lemon juice

[1] **Onion marmalade:** Peel and thinly slice the onions. Cook in olive oil with a pinch of salt over medium heat for about 30 minutes, letting them catch and caramelise at the bottom for colour and depth. Lower the heat, add the sugar, and cook for another 20 minutes. Deglaze with sherry vinegar and cook for 10 minutes more. Season with salt and lemon juice.

[2] **Smoked oil:** Place hay in a large pot with a smaller heatproof container of sunflower oil alongside. Ignite the hay with a blowtorch, immediately cover and seal with cling film. Infuse for at least 30 minutes.

[3] **Tempura batter:** Whisk the flour and cornstarch together. Gradually add the IPA and sparkling water until smooth. Season with salt and keep chilled.

[4] **Smoked sabayon:** Gently heat the egg yolks over low heat, whisking continuously until doubled in volume and around 65 °C. Remove from heat and slowly drizzle in the smoked oil, whisking until thick and smooth. Season with salt and lemon juice.

[5] **Asparagus:** Heat neutral oil to 180 °C. Trim the asparagus, dip in tempura batter, and fry for 1–2 minutes per side until crisp and golden. Drain and season immediately with salt and lemon juice.

[6] **To serve:** Spread onion marmalade on the plate, arrange the asparagus on top, and spoon the smoked sabayon over. Serve immediately.

CHEF'S NOTE

This is my signature dish — very simple but well-executed, with delicate flavours. I came across it during my first job as a chef at Les Pères Populaires, and I'll never forget the feeling of discovering my own personal style in cooking. At the restaurant, I source all my produce from Natoora, but at home I would choose the asparagus from Épicerie Berrie: they have the best produce and very friendly staff. For additional crunch, I like to add crispy shallots. It makes the dish even more complete.

Stuffed Duck's Neck Sausage & Caramelised Apple Purée (57)

Ideal for celebratory dinners with a rustic touch.

– Whole duck (breasts reserved for another dish)	1
– Chicken livers	100 g
– Pork shoulder, cut into small pieces	300 g
– Pistachios, toasted and chopped	50 g
– Parsley, bunch, finely chopped	1
– Whole-grain mustard	2 tbsp
– Olive oil	2 tbsp
– Large Golden apples, quartered and cored	5
– Cognac	50 g
– Powdered sugar	150 g
– Rosemary sprig	1
– Salt	
– Black pepper	
– Sherry vinegar	

[1] **Duck:** Butcher the duck, separating the wings, breasts, and legs. Set aside the carcass for stock and the breasts for another dish. If you're not comfortable butchering, ask your butcher to do it for you. Reserve the livers, hearts, and all trimmings from the wings.

[2] **Meat:** Rinse the chicken livers in cold water and pat them dry. Cut the pork shoulder into smaller pieces to fit through a meat grinder.

[3] **Duck neck:** Carefully remove the neck bone, ensuring the skin remains intact. Use scissors to trim any chewy bits inside.

[4] **Sausage filling:** Grind the pork shoulder, chicken livers, duck hearts, and wing trimmings. Mix with pistachios, parsley, mustard, olive oil, and sherry vinegar. Season with salt and pepper. Fry a small portion in a pan to taste-test and adjust seasoning if needed.

[5] **Apple purée:** Preheat the oven to 220 °C (428 °F). Toss the apple quarters with salt, cognac, sherry vinegar, and powdered sugar. Roast for 20 minutes until caramelised. Blend into a smooth purée and set aside.

[6] **Neck stuffing:** Transfer the sausage mixture into a piping bag. Carefully stuff the duck neck in one go to avoid air pockets. Tie the open end with kitchen twine.

[7] **Sausage:** Lower the oven temperature to 110 °C (230 °F). Rub the stuffed neck with olive oil, salt, and pepper. Place in a roasting pan with a sprig of rosemary and roast for 40 minutes without ventilation.

[8] **To serve:** Heat a pan over medium heat and sear the sausage until the skin is crisp. Slice and serve with the apple purée.

CHEF'S NOTE

I like to have my stuffing sit in a fridge at least overnight for deepening the flavours. Autumn is a perfect season for this dish.

Zacharie Gannat

Chef

Zacharie is a French chef celebrated for his instinctive and liberated approach to cooking. Originally on course to become an engineer, he pivoted into gastronomy and trained under notable mentors before carving out his own identity. His signature style often features just three ingredients on a plate, combining precision, depth and unexpected pairings. He credits the simple snack his grandmother used to make him (alphabet-shaped pasta in warm milk with sugar) as the reason he cooks the way he does today. For him, cooking is a language — a way to share emotion, memories and energy without speaking; it feels alive, like a conversation, with the ultimate goal of reaching something honest in the people who eat his food.

@ZAACTHESNACK

Quick-Fire Question Round

Sweet or Savoury?

Surf, Turf or Greens?

Pasta or Rice?

Gourmet or Street Eats?

Baked, Fried or Grilled?

What is your go-to comfort food and why?
Definitely the xiao long bao from Royal China in Paris (3rd). Asian food has always been something deeply special to me — I love it in a way that's hard to explain. Every time I eat those dumplings, something happens. It's the MSG, the broth, the setting — there's just a kind of magic in that mix.

What's a staple ingredient in your fridge?
There's always a bottle of Kewpie mayo in my fridge. That slightly sesame-leaning industrial mayo is my guilty pleasure. I use it way too easily — on sandwiches, eggs, whatever. It just makes everything taste a bit happier.

What do you love about the food scene in your city?
What I love about the food scene in Paris is that the level is incredibly high — you can eat really well at almost any price point. But more than that, there's a real sense of kindness and support among people in the industry. That atmosphere makes it a genuinely special place to cook and to live.

What is a dish that everyone should try at least once?
The pizettes at Café du Coin! Honestly, they have the best quality-to-price ratio in Paris.

What is one thing you wish people understood about your culture's cuisine?
I wish people understood that my culture's cuisine isn't about rules, it's about emotion. It's not only technique or tradition; it's the feeling behind what we cook. The best food from my culture isn't rigid or formal. It's generous, alive and deeply human. It's meant to make you feel something, not just impress you.

Photo by
Mickael Bandassak

Artichoke, Warm Vinaigrette & Limequat (58)

A bright yet composed balance of warmth and vibrant acidity.

– Artichoke	1
– Limequats	2
– Egg yolk	1
– Trout roe	1 tbsp
– Leftover fig leaf oil	
– Unsalted butter	20 g
– Breadcrumbs	10 g
– Samphire	10 g
– Whole eggs	2
– Orange	1
– Limes	2
– Crushed hazelnuts	2
– White wine, glass	1
– Sunflower oil	100 g

[1] **Artichoke:** Turn the artichoke, cut in half, and steam until tender — the knife should slide in easily. Set aside to cool slightly.

[2] **Pan grattato:** Melt the butter in a small pan, add the breadcrumbs, and toast until golden brown, stirring constantly. Drain on kitchen paper to remove excess fat and keep crisp.

[3] **Warm citrus vinaigrette:** Whisk together the yolks from the whole eggs, a pinch of salt, the white wine, and the orange and lime juice in a saucepan. Heat gently, whisking continuously, until the mixture begins to thicken. Slowly incorporate the sunflower oil as you would for a light mayonnaise, until creamy. Keep warm.

[4] **To serve:** Arrange the artichoke halves on the plate and spoon over the warm vinaigrette. Add the pan grattato, samphire, egg yolk, trout roe, crushed hazelnuts, and a few limequat wedges. Finish with a touch of fig leaf oil for aroma.

CHEF'S NOTE

Everyone knows the classic steamed artichoke with vinaigrette in the middle — this is a fun twist where the artichoke is cold and the vinaigrette is warm. Wear gloves when trimming the artichokes, otherwise your fingers will turn black. You can also keep the peeled artichokes in lemon water before cooking to prevent them from oxidising.

Mozzarella di Bufala, Fig Leaf Oil & Raspberry Powder (59)

An inspired choice for light, luxurious entertaining.

- AOP Mozzarella di Bufala — 1
- Sunflower oil — 100 g
- Fig leaves — 5
- Raspberry powder

[1] Heat the sunflower oil to 85 °C (185 °F).

[2] Pour the hot oil over the fig leaves, cut into quarters.

[3] Blend for about 10 minutes to fix the chlorophyll and extract the aroma.

[4] Strain through a cloth or coffee filter for a clear, fragrant green oil.

[5] Generously pour the fig leaf oil onto the plate.

[6] Place half a tempered and lightly salted mozzarella on top.

[7] Sprinkle with raspberry powder for a bright, tangy finish.

[8] Enjoy immediately.

Note: To make your own raspberry powder, dehydrate fresh raspberries, blend them, then sift to obtain a fine powder.

CHEF'S NOTE

What really makes the difference is tempering the mozzarella properly. When you cut it in half, make sure to blot it — that way, the whey doesn't spread everywhere.

Fresh Corn Polenta, Spider Crab & Bisque (60)

A dish that captures warmth with refined intensity.

– Live spider crab	1
– Unsalted butter	20 g
– Chives, bunch	1
– White wine, glass	1
– White onion	1
– Tomato paste	1 tsp
– Celery stalk	1/4
– Fresh corn on the cob	2

[1] **Spider crab:** Bring a large pot of salted water to a boil. Cook the live spider crab for 1 minute per 50 g of its weight. Once cooked, let it cool completely. Carefully remove all the meat and keep the shells for the bisque. Refrigerate the crab meat until serving.

[2] **Bisque:** In a hot, lightly greased saucepan, sauté the spider crab shells until well browned. Deglaze with the white wine, then add the aromatic garnish (onion, tomato paste, celery). Cover with water just to the top of the ingredients and simmer gently for 3 hours. Strain the broth and reduce it over medium heat until it reaches a thick, glossy, coating consistency.

[3] **Fresh corn polenta:** Using a box grater (coarse side), grate the kernels from the corn cobs. In a hot saucepan, melt 10 g of butter until foamy, then add the grated corn. Whisk continuously until the texture becomes creamy and slightly runny, like soft scrambled eggs. Remove from heat, add the remaining 10 g of butter, and season to taste.

[4] **To serve:** If you've kept the crab shell, use it as a natural serving bowl, otherwise a deep plate works perfectly. Spoon in the fresh corn polenta, top generously with crab meat, and pour over the hot bisque. Finish with a sprinkle of finely chopped chives. Serve immediately and enjoy the balance between the sweetness of the corn, the depth of the bisque, and the freshness of the crab.

CHEF'S NOTE

Keep the fresh corn polenta cold in the fridge or on ice before cooking. It helps create a thermal shock, and the flavour becomes noticeably sweeter. Also, weighing your spider crab really makes a difference for the quality of the cooking.

In a city where there is something for everyone, the best eateries and bars are often the ones that do not try too hard to be noticed. From cosy bistros and low-lit brasseries to lively spaces filled with regulars who know exactly what to order, the following picks are not about what is fashionable, but about what feels right — places that locals return to again and again for the welcome (as much as the wine!).

Tastemakers' Tables

An insider's food guide

Kamo

$

Kamo offers a tight but thoughtful menu that celebrates bold Japanese flavours in an intimate, eight-seat counter setting. Enjoy honest, modern takes on classics like the beef udon, vegetarian ramen and fried chicken burger — plus excellent wine recommendations and homemade churros.

17 Rue Martel, 75010 Paris
@kamo_paris

BÀNỘI

$

BÀNÔI was founded by My-Ly Pham in tribute to her grandmother ("bà nội" in Vietnamese). Drawing on her travels across Southeast Asia, the menu brings together familiar and comforting flavours from the region in original, homemade recipes. Its specialty is the Vietnamese spring roll, served as a main dish and enjoyed with sides like Thai coconut soup, bánh mi bites and a glass of white wine. Everything is prepared fresh in-house using produce from the nearby market.

For street food savoir faire with an authentic home-made feel

129 Rue Amelot, 75011 Paris
51 Rue des Vinaigriers, 75010 Paris
(Amelot) +33 1 71 93 48 75
(Vinaigriers) +33 1 83 87 47 82
banoi.fr

OTÉ

$

OTÉ celebrates the generous, spicy, and fragrant flavours of Réunion in a hip and friendly atmosphere. Known for its fiery house hot sauce, it serves vibrant Creole cuisine with a street-food twist, where diners can choose between sandwich or tray formats. Try the rougail saucisses or samoussas for a true taste of the island and wash it all down with a rum cocktail or two. Vegetarian, vegan, halal, gluten-free, and lactose-free options are available.

46 Rue Jean-Pierre Timbaud, 75011 Paris
+33 6 65 55 27 51
ote-restaurant.com

© Lara Carlon

Pistil

Pistil serves vibrant, market-driven vegetarian cuisine inside Ménagerie de Verre, a landmark contemporary arts venue in the city. Locals go for its generous, flavour-packed lunches that are refined, seasonal, and surprisingly affordable.

- 12 Rue Lechevin, 75011 Paris
- +33 6 51 34 45 92
- pistil.paris

Distrito Francés

Serving Mexican soul food with a French touch, Distrito Francés welcomes you with tacos and margaritas in a vibrant atmosphere.

- (DF Marais) 25 Rue du Pont Aux Choux, 75003 Paris
- (DF Saint Martin) 10 Rue du Faubourg Saint-Martin, 75010 Paris
- (DF Marais) +33 1 43 37 26 62
- (DF Saint Martin) +33 7 88 05 22 39
- distritofrances.fr

Project Sausage

Project Sausage is the first British deli in Paris serving handmade classics and comfort food like hot sandwiches, sausage rolls, pork pies, and Cornish pasties — all baked fresh daily using locally sourced ingredients.

- 57 Rue du Chemin Vert, 75011 Paris
- +33 6 68 71 75 95
- projectsausage.com

Sandwichette

Sandwichette is a charming, one-of-a-kind sandwich shop that reimagines classic French cuisine in creative, gourmet sandwich form. Its chicken-bacon sandwich is a favourite among the lunch crowd, alongside vegetarian options and homemade sides.

- 52 Rue Saint Maur, 75011 Paris
- sandwichette.com

© Salomé Rateau

Le Jourdain

Le Jourdain is a lively, intimate bistro that celebrates fresh ingredients and innovative French cuisine. It offers a tapas-style menu designed for sharing, featuring high-quality dishes influenced by European, health-conscious cooking.

- 101 Rue Des Couronnes, 75020 Paris
- +33 1 43 66 29 10
- lejourdain.fr

Cantine by day, wine bar by night

Comptoir Club

Comptoir Club is an all-day bistro where everything is thoughtfully prepared in-house. From breakfast in the morning to a regularly changing lunch menu, its cuisine reflects both the seasons and the team's inspiration. In the afternoon, diners can pause for coffee and a selection of homemade pastries. As evening settles in, the atmosphere becomes more convivial — with sharing plates accompanied by natural and conventional wines, cocktails, and more.

Pets are welcome!

56 Rue Amelot, 75011 Paris
+33 1 73 74 74 72
comptoirclub.fr

© The Travel Buds

Maslow Temple

Maslow Temple is a lively spot known for its creative, largely plant-based cooking and globally inspired flavours. Its seasonal, share-friendly menu includes creative options like the Not Boring Salad with red cabbage and apple. Expect a convivial atmosphere with warm service and reasonable prices for the neighbourhood — ideal for relaxed brunches and cocktail-fuelled evenings.

32 Rue de Picardie, 75003 Paris
maslow-restaurants.com

Kodawari Ramen (Tsukiji)

Kodawari Ramen (Tsukiji) brings the spirit of Tokyo's legendary fish market to Paris with a seafood-focused take on Japanese ramen. Inspired by Tsukiji's energy and abundance, the menu highlights broths built around fish and shellfish, using carefully sourced ingredients and house-made noodles crafted from specially milled wheat. Try the Tsukiji Special Ramen, a rich seafood broth topped with fresh fish and Japanese ingredients that capture the vibrant soul of the market.

Awarded a Bib Gourmand

12 Rue Richelieu, 75001 Paris
+33 1 42 61 34 60
kodawari-ramen.com

Le Coyote

Le Coyote is a queer saloon and an inclusive space for the LGBTQIA+ community and friends. Blending coffee shop, restaurant, and bar, it serves natural wines, bourbon, and American-inspired plates in a warm, western-tinged setting.

86 Rue des Archives, 75003 Paris
+33 7 82 06 43 06
@lecoyoteparis

Wani

Wani is a Japanese-French café renowned for its beautifully crafted dishes, matcha, and refined pastries. A cosy hidden gem with limited seating that gets busy during lunch, it also offers a curated range of products that make for charming souvenirs.

7 ter Rue Saint-Placide, 75006 Paris
waniparis.com

Bistrot Darsy

Bistrot Darsy channels old-school Paris with its vintage crockery and classic menu. Enjoy French auberge staples—terrine, celery rémoulade, roast chicken, steak tartare, and escargots—alongside thoughtful vegetarian dishes.

15 Rue des Panoyaux, 75020 Paris
+33 1 43 58 45 45
bistrotdarsy.fr

Coretta

Coretta offers seasonal bistronomic cuisine through thoughtfully composed plates, elegant sauces, and modern interpretations of classic flavours, served with warmth and finesse.

- 151 B rue Cardinet 151 Bis rue Cardinet, 75017 Paris
- +33 1 42 26 55 55
- restaurantcoretta.com

Le Cheval d'Or

Le Cheval d'Or showcases contemporary Chinese cuisine with refined technique and robust flavours. Enjoy beautifully plated sharing dishes, delicate dumplings, seasonal vegetables, and inventive sauces in a sleek, understated setting.

- 21 Rue de la Villette, 75019 Paris
- +33 7 45 11 16 47
- chevaldorparis.com

Le Grand Bain

Le Grand Bain is a lively neighbourhood restaurant known for its seasonal plates and natural wines. Go for its creative sharing dishes with grilled vegetables, crudo, house charcuterie, and inventive desserts.

- 14 Rue Denoyez, 75020 Paris
- +33 9 83 02 72 02
- legrandbainparis.com

NEONATO

NEONATO is an Italian trattoria bringing a slice of contemporary Italy to Paris with a focus on handmade pasta, generous plates, and a lively, design-forward atmosphere. The menu celebrates comforting flavours such as silky fresh pasta, rich ragù, seasonal vegetables, and indulgent desserts — paired with a thoughtful selection of natural and Italian wines. Stylish yet approachable, it is made for relaxing dinners, shared dishes, and a vibrant crowd.

Offers authentic Neapolitan cuisine

- 182 Rue Saint-Martin, 75003 Paris
- neonatoparis.com

Cendrillon

Not suitable for kids

Cendrillon offers a convivial dining experience centred on generous sharing plates. Cuisine-wise, it is a big mix of flavours from around the world — grounded in French seasonal, high-quality products. Diners often pair its bold offerings with frozen mezcalitas and large-format wines. Signature dishes on the menu include its renowned Los Passagios pork sando with caviar, alongside a rotating whole grilled fish of the week. During summer, its loud and lively atmosphere reaches its peak on the terrace.

50 Rue Piat, Paris
+33 6 84 05 89 54
restaurantcendrillon.fr

© Lucile Derveaux

Brasserie Martin

Brasserie Martin channels the timeless spirit of a Parisian brasserie with a warm and contemporary buzz. Doors open at noon and the room quickly fills with a lively mix of neighbourhood regulars, stylish locals, and in-the-know visitors. Its rotisserie is a highlight—golden, juicy and flavourful—alongside classics like pâté en croûte, escargots, tartare, and sausage-purée. Complement your meal with something from the thoughtfully curated, well-priced wine list.

24 Rue Saint-Ambroise, 75011 Paris
+33 1 48 05 34 36
lanouvellegarde.com/en/brasserie-martin

Trâm 130

Trâm 130 is an intimate 25-seat bistro from French-Vietnamese chef Priscilla Trâm — blending French technique with Southeast Asian flair. Its seasonal, bistronomic plates range from marrow-topped beef tartare to miso aubergine and lacquered meats, which have earned praise for their full-bodied, creative flavours. Refined yet vibrant, it is a compelling destination for modern fusion dining in the city.

130 Rue Saint-Maur, 75011 Paris
@tramtramtramtramtram

Déviant

Déviant is a lively natural wine bar founded by chef Pierre Touitou. With its minimalist design centred around a marble counter and open kitchen, it serves sharp, seasonal small plates featuring market veggies, cured fish, and inventive snacks — paired with an extensive selection of wines. Casual, buzzy, and unapologetically vibrant, it is a go-to for exuberant evenings.

Celebrated for its alternative approach to traditional dining

© Arnaud Pyvka

39 Rue des Petites Écuries, 75010 Paris
deviant.paris

Café du Coin

Café du Coin offers a relaxed, neighbourhood bistro experience with seasonal French cooking. Expect creative specials and comforting dishes like freshly-baked pizzettes, caillette, and blood sausage at reasonable prices all day long.

9 Rue Camille Desmoulins, 75011 Paris
+33 1 48 04 82 46
@cafe_du_coin

À La Biche au Bois

À La Biche au Bois delivers a lively, old-school Parisian bistro experience centred on generous, meat-forward classics and seasonal game at excellent value. Enjoy its standout coq au vin, house-made terrines, and crisp frites.

45 Avenue Ledru-Rollin, 75012 Paris
+33 1 43 43 34 38
alabicheaubois.fr

Le Servan

Le Servan blends French techniques with subtle Asian influences. Tuck into bold seasonal plates amid a lively atmosphere and explore its wine list for unique, small-producer discoveries.

32 Rue Saint-Maur, 75011 Paris
+33 1 55 28 51 82
leservan.fr

Michelin Guide selection!

© Jordan Sapally

Pristine

Named after the old French word for "légumes anciens" as in heirloom vegetables, Pristine champions produce-driven cooking in the heart of Paris. Indulge in hyperlocal, shareable dishes with natural wines and artisanal spirits — where the menu evolves according to what nearby producers harvest.

8 Rue de Maubeuge, 75009 Paris
+33 9 55 67 47 54
pristineparis.com

Fimmina Pizzeria

$$

Led by Sicilian chef Davide Luca, Fimmina Pizzeria has been ranked among the world's 50 best pizzerias. Known for its 72-hour slow-fermented dough and organic ingredients, it pairs Neapolitan tradition with refined Italian elegance in both flavour and presentation. Signature pizzas like the Loren with 'nduja and stracciatella, and the pistachio-topped Cucinotta stand out alongside its Italian wines, tiramisu, and babà al limoncello.

For pizzas crafted to tell stories and honour influential women

- 43 Rue Laffitte, 75009 Paris
- +33 9 54 16 20 34
- fimmina-pizzeria.fr

© Michael Condran

Quedubon

Quedubon is a beloved neighbourhood bistro that specialises in offal, reflecting its chef Ollie Clarke's nose-to-tail philosophy. Its chalkboard menu changes with the seasons, showcasing honest and generous French comfort classics alongside signature dishes such as the award-winning veal tongue pastrami with relish and 16-hour confit beef cheek. Its approach is unfussy but precise, grounded in quality produce and solid technique. With a well-curated wine list and an easy, lived-in atmosphere, it is well suited to relaxed lunches and unhurried dinners.

Michelin Guide selection

22 Rue du Plateau, 75019 Paris
+33 1 42 38 18 65
restaurantquedubon.fr

Lissit

Lissit pairs seasonal cuisine with house-made charcuterie, living wines, vermouths, and cocktails. Diners can expect refined yet relaxed dining that balances culinary precision with late-night energy.

48 Rue de la Folie Mericourt, 75011 Paris
+33 1 80 87 22 68
barlissit.com

Fugue

Fugue offers a delightful dining experience focused on inventive, seasonal plates with precise technique and vibrant flavours. Go for its quality-driven, fairly priced weekday lunch menu with wine from the thoughtful list.

128 Rue du Faubourg Saint-Martin, 75010 Paris
+33 9 54 94 96 68
fugueparis.fr

Frenchie Bar à Vins

Frenchie Bar à Vins is a no-reservations wine bar designed with sharing in mind. Open nightly, its epicurean cuisine blends original creations with reinvented classics — to be enjoyed with a wide selection of wines by the glass.

6 Rue du Nil, 75002 Paris
+33 1 40 39 96 19 9
frenchie-bav.com

© Virginie Garnier

Le Baratin

Le Baratin reimagines French bistro tradition with subtle South American touches — balancing delicate and hearty flavours. Enjoy expertly prepared meats, vibrant seasonal vegetables and curated wines served in a lively, intimate setting.

3 Rue Jouye-Rouve, 75020 Paris
+33 1 43 49 39 70
@lebaratinparis

L'Orient d'Or

L'Orient d'Or has been serving regional Chinese cuisine since 2005. Expect generous plates designed for sharing: smoked pork, clay-pot cabbage, noodles with real depth, and dishes that don't shy away from heat.

22 Rue de Trévise, 75009 Paris
+33 1 48 00 07 73
lorientdor.fr

Elbi

Elbi offers a distinct and contemporary dining experience rooted in seasonal French cuisine with nuanced international accents. Diners can indulge in artfully plated dishes with delicately cured fish, slow-cooked meats, and colourful vegetable compositions, shaped by what's in season. A focused tasting menu and carefully curated wines make it a destination for elegant yet unpretentious evenings.

54 Rue de Paradis, 75010 Paris
+33 1 42 26 40 14
restaurantelbi.fr

© Ilya Kagan

© Ludovic Balay

Tempête

$$$

Tempête stands out for its surprise tasting format and ever-changing menu shaped entirely by the market. The compact, counter-style setting creates an immersive, chef-close experience that feels spontaneous, lively, and distinctly contemporary. Rather than following strict traditions, its dishes lean toward fusion influences — with a focus on bold, well-defined flavours. It is an ideal destination for those seeking something spirited and slightly off-beat within the city's dining scene.

© Ludovic Balay

5 Cour des Petites Écuries, 75010 Paris
+33 9 70 66 74 96
tempeteparis.fr

Délicatisserie

$$$

Délicatisserie is a high-end pastry boutique created by Nina Métayer, dedicated to limited-edition, seasonally inspired entremets crafted with expert technique and layered textures. Collections are released in curated drops and can be pre-ordered, reflecting a couture approach to pâtisserie. Expect intricate flavour pairings, unexpected infusions, and architectural finishes.

Nina is the first woman to be named World's Best Pastry Chef (2024)

Printemps Homme (8th floor), Printemps Haussmann, 64 Boulevard Haussmann, 75009 Paris
+33 1 42 82 40 02
delicatisserie.com

© Théodore Meira

Pétrelle

$$$

Pétrelle is an intimate, chef-driven restaurant offering meticulously crafted seasonal cuisine in a limited-table setting. Its thoughtful tasting menu highlights include white asparagus, Breton fish, and delicately balanced desserts.

34 Rue Petrelle, 75009 Paris
+33 1 42 82 11 02
petrelle.fr

Vantre

$$$

Vantre is a Parisian bistro dedicated to seasonal French cooking with a modern edge. Expect refined plates shaped by market produce and a remarkable cellar focused on artisanal growers for thoughtful food-and-wine pairings.

19 Rue de la Fontaine au Roi, 75011 Paris
+33 1 48 06 16 96
vantre.fr

Le Sévero

$$$

Le Sévero has championed exceptional beef since 1987. Celebrating tradition, craftsmanship, and the art of butchery, its signature dishes include dry-aged côte de bœuf, classic tartare with house fries, and veal head croustillant.

8 Rue des Plantes, 75014 Paris
+33 1 45 40 40 91
lesevero.com

Awarded a Bib Gourmand

Le Cornichon $$$

Le Cornichon is a convivial neighbourhood bistro devoted to generous, seasonally driven French cuisine. Expect hearty classics, thoughtful daily specials, and carefully sourced ingredients prepared with restraint and flavour in mind.

- 2 Rue des Goncourt, 75011 Paris
- +33 1 42 54 18 32
- lecornichon.paris

© Felix Dol Maillot

Le Dauphin $$$

Le Dauphin is a sleek, marble-clad tapas bar known for inventive small servings and a serious natural wine focus. Favourites include delicate seafood preparations, bold vegetable dishes, and creative offal plates.

- 131 Ave Parmentier, 75011 Paris
- +33 1 55 28 78 88
- restaurantledauphin.net

Restaurant Alan Geaam $$$$

Alan Geaam showcases refined French cuisine infused with Lebanese heritage, creating a distinctive, cross-cultural dining experience.

- 19 Rue Lauriston, 75016 Paris
- +33 1 45 01 72 97
- alangeaam.fr

© Marie Monsieur

Restaurant MAISON $$$$

Restaurant MAISON presents a contemporary tasting-menu experience shaped by French foundations and Japanese nuance. Its cuisine moves fluidly between delicate seafood, thoughtfully prepared vegetables, and gently layered broths and sauces, reflecting a seasonal, market-driven approach. In its serene, minimalist dining room, each meal unfolds with elegant rhythm and balance — offering a subtle yet deeply expressive exploration of texture, aroma, and flavour.

- 3 Rue Saint-Hubert, 75011 Paris
- +33 1 43 38 61 95
- en.maison-sota.com

© Florian Domergue

Accents Table Bourse

$$$$

Awarded one Michelin star

24 Rue Feydeau, 75002 Paris
+33 1 40 39 92 88
accents-restaurant.com

Accents Table Bourse offers an elegant, contemporary dining experience built around refined French techniques and flavourful touches from around the globe. Go for the inventive tasting menu, where seafood meets citrus and spice, and seasonal vegetables are lifted by refined sauces. Its modern yet intimate space and polished service underscore the restaurant's precision, creativity, and quietly adventurous spirit.

© Florian Domergue

© Florian Domergue

Terra

Terra is a convivial French restaurant in the Haut Marais where wood-fired grilling defines the menu. Designed for sharing, dishes range from dry-aged meats and delicately seared fish to inventive vegetarian creations — all cooked over open flame in a visible kitchen. A lush glass-roofed dining room and cellar of 1,000+ natural wines make it a memorable evening destination.

21 Rue des Gravilliers, 75003 Paris
+33 1 45 30 02 58
terraparis.fr

Ojii

Ojii is a contemporary Japanese restaurant in Paris that reimagines izakaya culture with refined technique and premium ingredients. Indulge in expertly sliced sashimi, delicate tempura, and standout wagyu dishes, alongside rare Japanese whiskies and saké. Its sleek, intimate space near the Eiffel Tower makes it an appealing stop for travellers seeking polished yet vibrant dining.

An atmospheric space inspired by "In the Mood for Love"

6 Rue Perronet, 75007 Paris
+33 1 45 38 53 99
ojii.fr

Red Katz

$$$$

Red Katz is a contemporary Paris restaurant blending French techniques with Asian influences. Its creative, seasonally evolving plates, precise sauces, and bold flavour contrasts are presented in a sleek, intimate space where counter seating and creative cocktails add to its modern, detail-driven dining experience.

Where classic Chinese flavours meet modern French flair

- 14 Rue de Cléry, 75002 Paris
- +33 7 49 71 91 13
- redkatz.fr

Restaurant Omar Dhiab

$$$$

Restaurant Omar Dhiab presents refined French cooking infused with subtle Tunisian influences. Its tasting menus highlight seafood and beautifully handled vegetables, often layered with gentle spice and citrus. The restaurant's minimalist, softly lit interior creates an intimate, almost serene atmosphere that makes it a compelling destination for quietly distinctive meals.

- 23 Rue Hérold, 75001 Paris
- +33 1 42 33 52 47
- omardhiab.com

© Virgine Garnier

Plénitude

$$$$

Plénitude redefines haute cuisine through an obsessive, poetic focus on sauce. Conceived as intricate absolutes, these perfume-like creations are blended from complex aromas and elevate any dish from seafoods, meats, and desserts alike. Set in an intimate first-floor dining room in the Cheval Blanc Paris overlooking the Seine, the experience feels like a choreographed, sensory journey through France's finest landscapes.

Awarded (3) Michelin stars

Cheval Blanc Paris, 8 Quai du Louvre, 75001 Paris
+33 1 79 35 50 11
chevalblanc.com/fr/maison/paris/restaurants-et-bars/plenitude

Le Rigmarole

$$$$

Le Rigmarole is a lively Franco-Japanese spot where yakitori takes centre stage. Enjoy expertly grilled skewers cooked over binchotan charcoal, handmade udon, and vibrant small plates — all served in a relaxed, counter-style setting.

10 Rue de Grand-Prieuré, 75011 Paris
+33 1 71 24 58 44
lerigmarole.com

© Jordan Sapally

Vivide

$$$$

Vivide is a fine-dining restaurant offering creative, seasonally inspired cuisine. Expect refined plates built around vibrant produce, precise technique, and balanced flavours, alongside a thoughtful wine selection.

3 Rue Dancourt, 75018 Paris
+33 1 42 58 00 11
vivide-paris.com

Dedicated to hyper-local and creative plant-based cuisine

© Juan Jerez

De Vie

$$$$

De Vie is a modern Parisian cocktail bar and restaurant that pairs inventive, seasonal plates with cocktails celebrating local French produce and producers. Its menu is guided by a strong zero-waste ethos, with fermentation and preservation techniques at its heart. An energetic, design-forward space and creative tasting menus make it a lively destination for curious travellers.

© Juan Jerez

22-24 Rue Saint-Sauveur, Paris
devie.bar

© Offside

Frenchie

$$$$

Awarded one Michelin star

Frenchie is a warmly intimate restaurant where chef Greg Marchand lets the seasons write the script. Its five-course carte blanche menu moves fluidly between French techniques and global influences, guided entirely by the produce. Precise cooking, textured plates, and thoughtful wine pairings define the dining experience, while its two Écotable macarons reflect a genuine commitment to responsible gastronomy.

5 Rue du Nil, 75002 Paris
+33 1 40 39 96 19 9
frenchie-ruedunil.com

erh

$$$$

Housed within La Maison du Saké, erh unites Japanese technique and French terroir in refined, seasonal tasting menus. Thoughtful saké pairings deepen the experience, which continues at Golden Promise — the vaulted bar downstairs.

- 11 Rue Tiquetonne, 75002 Paris
- +33 1 45 08 49 37
- restaurant-erh.com

Septime

$$$$

Septime captures the spirit of modern Parisian dining with its seasonal, produce-forward tasting menus and effortlessly cool atmosphere. Dishes are meticulously made yet vibrant, spotlighting vegetables, seafood, and natural wines.

- 80 Rue de Charonne, 75011 Paris
- +33 1 43 67 38 29
- septime-charonne.fr

Le Clarence

$$$$

Le Clarence delivers grand, theatrical French gastronomy in a lavish 19th-century mansion near the Champs-Élysées. Expect richly composed tasting menus, intricate sauces, and opulent interiors that feel both aristocratic and intimate.

- 31 Avenue Franklin Delano Roosevelt, 75008 Paris
- +33 1 82 82 10 10
- le-clarence.paris

Awarded 2 Michelin stars

Mosuke

$$$$

Mosuke is a bold, haute-cuisine restaurant that brings together African, Japanese, and French influences in a singular, ever-evolving expression. Opened in 2020, it unfolds as a sensory experience shaped by more than 300 house infusions and fermentations. Signature dishes such as the Pepe Soup with kombu-katsuobushi broth and the shea-butter-aged Beef Mafé reveal a cuisine layered with spice, memory, and precision.

- 11 Rue Raymond Losserand, 75014 Paris
- +33 1 43 20 21 39
- mosuke-restaurant.com

CITIx60 RECIPES: PARIS

First published and distributed by
viction workshop ltd.

victionary™

viction workshop ltd.
Unit C, 7/F, Seabright Plaza,
9–23 Shell Street,
North Point, Hong Kong SAR
Url: www.victionary.com
Email: we@victionary.com

@victionworkshop
@victionworkshop
Bē @victionary
@victionary
小红书 @Victionary Books

Edited and produced by viction workshop ltd.
Creative Direction: Victor Cheung
Design: Hazan Yeung, Scarlet Ng
Editorial: YL Lim, Ynes Filleul
Coordination: Jeanie Choy, Katherine Wong
Production: Bryan Leung

Illustration: Alice May (A Does Art)

Typefaces: Aeonik Fono Pro (Regular, Medium) Aeonik Pro (Regular, Medium) by CoType® Foundry, PP Kyoto (Light, Regular, Regular Italic, Medium, Semibold, Bold) by Pangram Pangram®, Raim Standard Light, Raim Display Light Italic by Lift Type

ISBN 978-988-70661-2-5
Printed and bound in China

Acknowledgements
We would like to thank all the designers, studios, and companies who were involved in the production of this book for their significant contribution to its compilation. We would also like to express our gratitude to all the producers involved for their invaluable opinions and assistance, as well as the professionals in the creative industry who were generous with their insights and feedback throughout the entire production process. Last but not least, to those who made specific input behind the scenes but were not credited in this book, we acknowledge and appreciate all your effort and continuous support.

Future Editions
Want to be featured in our next CITIx60 Recipes project? Drop us a hello with your portfolio at: we@victionary.com